EVEN AS THE SOUL

Even as the Soul Prospers

James T. Freeman

Word Association Publishers
205 5th Avenue
Tarentum, Pennsylvania
www.wordassociation.com

Printed in the United States of America.

ISBN 10: 1-59571-147-3

ISBN 13: 978-1-59571-147-2

Library of Congress Control Number: 2006929361

Word Association Publishers

205 5th Avenue

Tarentum, PA 15084

www.wordassociation.com

Acknowledgments

I am grateful for a loving family, a praying mother Beverly A. Smith, siblings (Melissa Jackson, George Freeman Jr., and Erickka Wilson) all who make me feel like I can do anything, and a support network of friends. To my cousin Charles Herring, thanks for everything your help and support is priceless. John Robinson II, your friendship has been invaluable!

There are also those who have made significant contribution in the editing and reading process, Starla Williams, Jeanette Calhoun, Nicole Pugh, and Timoni Webster; thanks to each of you your help was much appreciated.

To my spiritual father Bishop Duane E. Youngblood. Your guidance, support, and encouragement have awakened the gift in me and have challenged me to dare to believe God at the next level. For this I will always be grateful. I am glad that God has allowed us to covenant together in this season where He is rapidly ushering the revelation of the Kingdom Son in the earth.

To the memory of my natural God father John Kinsel, thanks for letting me know the love of a son. Also to the memory of my nephew Robert James Freeman-thanks for demonstrating the truths of this book in your life and in your death… "We are not average!"

This book has gone through several shifts; I want to recognize the significant contributions of Dr. Gerald Loyd of the Fountain of Life Church International, the Higher Call World Outreach church family and A Second Chance Inc. family and friends…you guys mean more to me than you will ever know. Thanks for pulling out the best in me.

Dedication

To my wife, my love, my friend, words can not begin to describe my appreciation for your support, love and your commitment to my dreams, visions, ministry and the development of our children. I am grateful for your love. First, your love to God and how He allows you to love me out of your commitment to Him. My prayer always is that He continues to reveal to me how to love you as we continue our journey to grow together.

To my children, daddy loves both of you so much!

Joshua, you are my future. I pray that you come to know God for yourself and discover that what God has for you is better than any other offer you will encounter… and know that they will come. Stay close to this family's vision and pursue purpose…. Bring God Glory!

Madison, you are my joy. I pray that you find joy in knowing that God calls you friend. Know always that all you need is in Him and Him alone. Know and enjoy the pleasures of this life; but NEVER put more stock in them than you put in your faith and trust in God. Be Glory and exude Grace!

Contents

Foreword

"Even As the Soul", what a title and what a truth. When John wrote from the heart beat of God that he wished prosperity for all of us and connected it to the prosperity of the soul, he opened major doors that need to be revealed to us now more than ever. We are living in an age where we are trying to make it happen in any way possible. People are so without true peace and have not really concluded how to live a life with inner harmony. As you listen to the news or to the hearts of people you can see that our world is hurting and the pain goes to the soul. We, in America, have more than ever, yet violence, drug abuse and divorce still are high among us. We have bigger homes and fancier cars, only to still not really be inwardly happy. I know many possibly reading this book have had a very interesting journey to your today place, but the decision about your next steps may be uncertain. I believe like the author it is time for us **to consider the soul**. In a fallen man it becomes the real source of his living, and in a regenerated man it becomes the focus of his development. Whatever your state of life may be today you cannot afford to ignore the call for soul prosperity. We must move beyond what we have and see who we are if true prosperity is to come to us. This prosperity will require the individual spending time with God for in those moments true faith is imparted. By faith I mean the information, impartation and manifestation of God that causes us to possess the Kingdom benefits and promises of God. The longing and lost soul is absent of this faith because it has not been exposed to the heart and mind of the creator

When I consider a generation of broken homes, victims of abuse or neglect, I see a generation of wounded souls. The cry of those souls is heard every night across the globe when we see the violence played out day by day. A wounded person wounding others becomes a major theme in a society devoid of the true understanding about the necessary development of the soul. Our society has seen it all to often and it is time we move beyond the wounds and confusion of the soul. When we think about the mind, the will and emotions of a person we must know that the past experiences will be a great indicator of the future judgments. Without good material and without embracing a process the wounds will only continue.

When I consider all the material I have read over the past 20 years concerning personal growth and development or materials that cause the

Christian believer to move forward in the necessary processes of life, this book stands out to me as a thorough presentation that will propel the human soul. We are living in times where true prosperity is being defined so many ways, but the way in which James Freeman deals with such complicated concepts and makes them so easily understood will only enhance the life of any reader. After reading through his approach to the development of the soul, a necessary for true prosperity, I can honestly say, his insight is truly from God and cut through so many years of questions for so many. After reading such a book I am convinced you can be more versed in how to approach your life journey and you will feel an increased level of confidence about the next steps you may wish to take in your personal journey. It is clear that the life of the true worshipper is a life defined by the proximity to God, for truly worship is all about position and not action. So in this personal journey that we all must embrace, there is a requirement of coming close to the creator. It is here, true meaning will come to the gifts and abilities we all possess in varying degrees. James has taken one of the most difficult themes and makes it applicable to all of us. He has gotten within the mind of God concerning how we function and why we function the way we function and show us all how to find what we all long for and that is the true development of our souls.

As a leader, I have discovered that the issues addressed within the pages of this great writing, help people walk into being whom they were called to be without so much unnecessary outside interference. The development we must approach is so apparent within the pages and James takes the time to be open enough to let the reader see the necessary course. It is clear to me in my capacity that a soul wasted is a life wasted. I know that many in the world today have major questions about life and why things have been the way they have been. Well, I would say to them all if you only read one book on developing the real you and becoming the person you must be, this is the book to read. I can see the careful time taken by a masterful mind and hand of God to release such wisdom to the masses. I guarantee if you read "Even as the Soul" you will not regret the relatively small investment you had to make to withdraw the great results you will see in your life and in all those whom you share the principles of this book with. James has been used of God to do this one and this is one for the whole body of Christ or any person seeking to find meaning in life.

Bishop DEY

Preface

A Message from the Heart

THERE'S A PEACE

There's A Peace

There's a peace in God my savior
There's a peace in Him alone
There's a hope that springs eternal
In God the peace within my Soul
Creator of all things so wise and true
Before anything was there alone stood you
Not standing in physical form yet existing
A thing the mind may never comprehend
The lover of my soul
The keeper of all things sacred and true
A friend yet still God.

James T. Freeman
Copyright © 2005 jtt95 Music

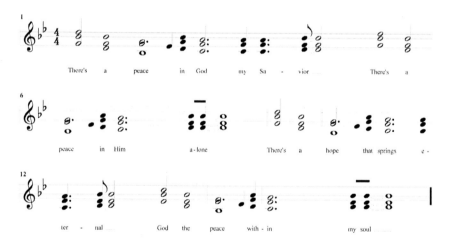

Even As the Soul....what an inspiration. There is such a God given talent in James as a Man of God, worshipper, social worker and clinician. This combination has prepared him to develop this book to provide readers with a framework to pinpoint their personal "soul journey". The spiritual discernment and understanding of human behavior has catapulted this book into existence.

Understanding processes of life whether the prospering of one's soul, one's walk through deliverance or defining one's life existence. James has opened the door for people to find a path and be at peace with the ever learning and developing soul. There is no quick fix. Put on your whole armor and with God's grace prepare to go to battle to find your soul's journey as you relate, laugh, and even cry as both natural and spiritual truths are written.

I am so proud of James' accomplishments and unbelievable faith. I have been blessed with heaven's best in a husband and the father of my children. This book is one of the ways in which James continues his soul journey and walks through healing as he shares with you.

Lachelle C. Freeman MA

I have been humbly privileged to provide prayerful support and editorial commentary to this premiere work of spiritual literature that will enrich your soul and lead to greater prosperity. Through its reading, I invite you to embark upon a journey of prayer, study and meditation towards a greater life of discipleship in Jesus Christ and fellowship with His children on earth. While I have been blessed by the manuscript, I have been more fulfilled in my study of the Word which has resulted from engaging the text that the author has artfully and thoughtfully penned. Inspired by years of experience as a social worker, therapist, minister of music and devoted family man, James Freeman's book has captured the essence of the mental musings of the mind.

There are those for whom intelligence is both a blessing of God and a curse of Satan. Who among us has not labored intently in failed and frustrating attempts to "figure things out"? Even those of us graced with the gift of salvation, often ponder the meaning of life amidst tragedy, despair, abuse, addiction, grief, mistakes, missteps, misgivings, and — yes, even sin. Thinking, for us, will not bring a sense of relief or release absent the Spirit of the living God. Hence, we must be guided by Biblical truths and spiritual principles in order to live in prosperity. As the author explains, prosperity is not inextricably tied to financial comfort or social acceptability; rather, the level of our prosperity corresponds directly to our spiritual conditioning.

As Christians, we know that we are saved, delivered, lifted, healed, comforted, and free. Yet, the reality of our circumstances requires that we are renewed and encouraged to prosper. This book, and its companion musical CD, brings renewal and encouragement for intellectuals, professionals and deep thinkers as "we are not ashamed of the Gospel of Jesus Christ." [Romans 1: 16]. Contrariwise, mental musings of the mind lead us to a place of infinite rest in our Lord and Savior when we allow His abiding Spirit to lead, guide and direct the development of our souls. Expect that your reading of this book will bring genuine joy, heartfelt hope and peaceful prosperity…as it has for my soul. We can exclaim together, "Return unto thy rest, O my soul; for the Lord hath dealt bountifully with thee." Psalm 116:7. Peace and Be Blessed, Starla Williams JD, LlM

Welcome to my personal journey. What I have found on my road to discover God in the earth is a truth, that once opened, continues to grow with each new day and experience. I have also settled the truths that the road to eternal peace with God is both full of joy and pain. In the process of writing this book and facing the ghost that accompanied, an unexpected and extremely difficult event occurred; my father died. The void of not having my father present in my life, but knowing that he was alive and literally in the same state, city, and community I lived in, but unable to have any type of relationship, was always a challenge for me to interpret. Above all, the thing that pained the most in our lack of relationship was just that, the absence of relationship. My father, James E. Peterson departed this life and I knew that I would never be the same. I felt that this experience was the final loss to something I had been losing all my life. Nevertheless, something inside me kept saying: *this is not the end but the beginning of yet another process.*

I was so mad and confused! I could not cry or feel what I felt everyone was expecting me to feel. I continued to ask God, "where is the view of the soul in all of this?" At the very last possible moment, I was called to the hospital. Already at the point of his death, my dad was lying there dying on life support. His eyes wide open, his body swollen from the strength of the medication and with no ability to communicate what I thought I wanted more than anything, had now been released to me. It was here and in this confusing situation, that I was now given the opportunity to partake in something I desired my whole life: time with my "dad." Not what I expected. However, I am grateful to God for permitting the time and space for it to occur. In an effort to hide from the pain of what was going on, I began to ask God; where was his soul? I knew that after death is judgment, but when does life cease for the individuals who, because of the sophisticated intervention of man, continue to live in the face of death? This to me was not life; it was only the maintaining of ones bodily functioning. It was hard to come to terms with this concept. My dad remained alive because his heart was pumping by the assistance of a machine. The doctors even cautioned us that if he were to become conscious, they would have to quickly sedate him due to the fact that he would be tremendously uncomfortable and in severe pain. The sophistication of mans gifts and abilities to manipulate and control events in the earth speak to a hidden talent in this earthly treasure created by the Father God in His image. The decision is to determine what I am going to do with this information; there remains this expectation in the earth for mature Christians to arise, take position and conquer in the office Jesus prepared in the earth. This is the greater works that we who believe and follow His teaching. I urge each reader to consider this truth; what God wants to do in the earth will depend on our availability and willingness. He is waiting on you to step into the office of a son in the earth and conquer with the mission to bring Him glory and honor. It is time for the true church to come out of hiding behind the walls of the temple and by our works, demonstrate the wisdom and power of God as He continues to speak with us in this modern age. Create the sound of God. There are people who wait for a sound that will awaken them from their slumbering positions, a people rotting away in a society that is advancing so rapidly without consideration of the ageless, truth that only what we do for Christ, will be counted in the end. This is a life of *meaning*; doing something for God through Christ.

In modern society we have it so mixed up. We view God and the Christian religion as a deterrent to our having and leading a fulfilled existence. How many of us have heard, "I am not going to be a Christian... there are just too many rules (those do's and don'ts)." Or even better, how many of us have said, "I can't go to church or think about commencing my Christian walk until I can get my life in order." The disheartening truth is that we fail to recognize that this event will never occur; we can not do anything without Him. How easily we start in the spirit and so quickly end up in the flesh. Strangely enough, we are so blinded to the principal that Christ is the source of our help, so why do we run away from our help at the point of need? Think about it. God does not desire to keep us from happiness; but to enhance your ability to experience true joy. He does this by providing meaning to your pain, suffering, and sorrow. He turns your tears into joy; your weeping into dancing; for the garment of praise is prepared for the spirit of heaviness. The key is simply to allow God, through his infinite wisdom and omnipotent power, to reveal his plan for your life. I constantly love to be reminded of God's sensitivity to us; how He knows and declares the end before the beginning. This to me is truly awesome that God in His foreknowledge predestined![1] The "Great One" planned around my failures, my excuses, my losses, my disappointments... the list could go on.

Even as the Soul is an opportunity, for the believer to take the heart aches, the struggles, and the learning experiences that they have gone through, in an attempt to make sense out of this life. It is also a tool in the hand of God to challenge each reader to do the work of discovering what God wanted from their life. This, in my opinion, is done when we begin to understand what He has called our family to; the searching out of the family gifts and talents. It is the opportunity to discover and work the thing the whole is known for. Further, I believe that God has deposited so much inside of me, for this season, as it pertains to the healing of the soul. I have discovered how the role of worship in the kingdom is closely related to the healing and growth of the soul. It is in worship to God that we encounter our vulnerabilities and weaknesses. We lay them down in reverence to a holy God, setting aside our agenda and desires to a higher purpose. This is the true worship the father seeks, worship occurring from the recognition of our inability to, in ourselves, offer an acceptable sacrifice. Paul encourages the believers to present their bodies as living sacrifices, but moves to the stage that is critical to the growth of the soul in admonishing the body to be transformed by the renewing of the mind. This is the growth we seek. The soul that declares with the scriptures, regardless of the test or the situation, I am determined to prove that which is good, acceptable, and the perfect will of God.[2] I believe that God is going to cause the believer to rise, in this current day, to a position in which the world will take note of the light that will shine forth declaring, *glory to God*. There will be a returning to the pursuit of His presence that will manifest in those who are seeking that will fulfill not only the longing soul, but will spill over, becoming a visible manifestation for all to observe the presence of the Lord in this day. Hear the warning, woe to those who are at ease in Zion. This is the time for us to arise. I believe that God will give an individual inner peace and wholeness. Once this occurs there is a greater real sense for the opportunity to grow. *Now* is the time, it is not the opportunity for us to pull back. We as

[1]Romans 8:29
[2]Romans 12:1-2

believers in this generation have reached the point where we can hear the challenge to be sons in the earth. However, it is necessary that we assume the position from the position of rest. God is not interested in what we can do in our own strength. He has been waiting for us to cease from our work. Science continues to prove that a person who is at peace (i.e. they have their life stressors under control and are able to cope, relax, etc...) has less health problems, better self care, and is happier. Therefore, it is imperative for Christians to realize, and begin to demonstrate to the world, true healing and health even in the midst of our weaknesses. The world has become so conditioned to our pretenses of health; nevertheless, I think we need to demonstrate to them our true self as believers. Do you believe all that He provided for us in His death? Declare, "I have healing and health... He was bruised for my transgression and sins." He was whipped that we might have health and beat that we might have peace. I urge you as believers to see the importance of your position in the earth once you truly accept that position as a Christian. We are His reflection. This is the manner of love that has been given to us.

It is my hope that from reading "Even as the Soul," everyone walks away with a dream. I pray that not just a dream, but faith and vision. My sincere belief is that God has purposed for every man/woman on earth the opportunity to discover meaning in their existence. It is this that will open the door and opportunity for them to have a deeper communication and connection with Him. Can't you see it? God is trying to show us something. He has never lost sight of the garden of rest He prepared for man, and in the recorded relationships with man He continues to point us to a God who desires to talk to us. Can you hear Him talking to Moses? Grow up in Pharaoh's house, be reared by his daughter, be schooled by his servants learn to rule and be priestly. Nevertheless, he would still have to meet his maker in the wilderness. There he would be humbled by the power of God, be introduced to the brokenness within himself, opened up to his insecurities and his inability, all for God to call and use him for the divine purpose of releasing Israel from Egypt. Hear again our God in dialogue with Abraham. Even this great warrior of faith had to embrace the process prior to receiving the promise. Examine the pain of having a wife who was barren, yet a word from God declaring you will bring forth.   Consider the challenge he and his wife faced in their effort to believe to receive Isaac; their promised child. After they received and nurtured the boy, only to hear God say, *return to me as a sacrifice the promise that I have given you.* Nonetheless, in his obedience he becomes the father to the nation and a patriarch of faith.

Listen in on the communication between God and Noah. This man, hearing the unheard, preparing for the unseen with special instruction by faith from God; he built an ark. He believed for salvation of his house in a time when there was no real threat of death and destruction. Can you believe for and receive secret information? God wants to talk with you, are you available to listen?

In each of the instances, we observe men of faith who were challenged to walk in an area that had no road map or prior individuals who had accomplished the task they were asked to perform.   Each of them demonstrated that learning to hear and obey God was a process; it wasn't simply He spoke and the task was accomplished. He provided insight here and there and as a relationship was built, revelation and information was revealed. Often many of us forget that it is in the everyday relationship that God seeks to develop our ability to hear and obey his voice. Many Christian believers are looking for that "big" opportunity to stand before God's people in the pulpit or the opportunity to work miracles of healing and deliverance in the prayer line; but God is simply waiting for us to learn to minister one to the other out of love.

Thoughts on Prosperity
When exploring the link between the growth of the soul and prosperity, the question arises, "What is in the link?" I guess for me the link is simply the understanding that our God is the supplier of all good and perfect gifts, He knows everything, and gives wisdom to get wealth.   Thus, once we enter into a relationship with Him, and through His love be given the opportunity to explore the "all" of who we are, we can give birth to our desires and dreams and be changed and released into the life He has called for us.   Provision for vision is promised to follow. It is my hope that the experience

of this book will challenge the believer to seek prosperity, not wealth. Seek relationship and the wisdom of God; natural wealth will follow and eternal rest will begin for you in your now. It is an awesome experience to know that He is challenging us to sit and eat, not to frantic activity to discover that which He already knows. How often we forget that our Father already knows the way we travel and what is "best" for us. So many of us, as believers, feel we need to work and explore things outside of our relationship with the Father to tap into the level of wealth and prosperity in this life. Not recognizing that He knows the number and magnitude of the talents He has released to us and will give to us the revelation of what His expectation is for us in the earth; but we must seek and ask.

So how do we reach prosperity as believers? It is the position of this writer that this occurs when the believers enters the rest of God and begins the journey of seeking the knowledge and wisdom of our creator. I guess the challenge of this understanding for many is, "what if in His will, the plan was not for me to obtain the lofty riches of this world?" I can only submit that we begin to challenge the thought and concept that equates God's blessing to material gain. I truly believe that these things will come once our focus is clear and on Him. He desires to give us good gifts; as we are His children. Consequently, as a good Father He knows what we can and can not bear. Remember the concept of stewardship—-He is not going to relinquish to us (to a degree) our inheritance simply to squander it foolishly if we have not adequately prepared to move and operate in the blessings. So begin to put things in order size up your talents and make a decision to seek God for the wisdom to get increase. Only He has the information we as believers need in regards to His purpose in our lives.

EVEN AS THE SOUL

Introduction

Can I See You Again?

Can I See You Again?

Can I see you again?
Can I see you again?
Can I see you again… this time through new eyes?
Don't want to hold you hostage to the things that I seen and heard before
Don't want to bind you to the realities of my past.
Don't want to hold you captive to the things my mind could not conceive
Or to the things my heart could not believe…
So, can I see you again… this time through new eyes?

James T. Freeman
Copyright © 2005 jtf95 Music

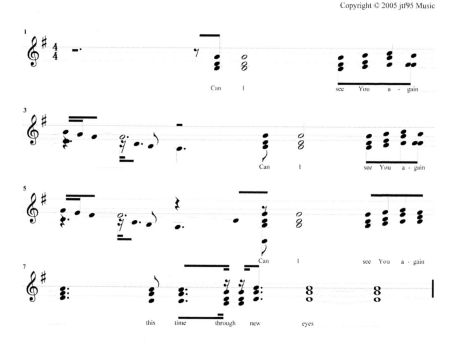

Discovering the Soul

For so long I have searched for a plan that would lead to security
I have waited and trusted in a faith I could not see
Sometimes doubting, never giving up hope, yet questioning - still holding on
Holding tight...
Always aware that He (God) is able
But faced with the reality that His ability depends on the power that is at
work in the "we"
Am I not willing? Is He not the force that exists to will... to do?
So, if He the God who is all-powerful and can do all things, cares then why
has He not chosen to do (The thing in my heart) ...for me?

In search of meaning in a world full of deception,
disappointment and despair, the human race continues
to struggle for truth or what will be adapted for this
book as the *purpose for being*. What is the key to this
understanding? What can guide us to a comprehensive
understanding of the truth of the human soul? More
importantly, should one continue in this quest, or
"relax" in the understanding that all that is needed will
be provided by the God who is all sufficient and the
supplier of all that is needed and desired? The journey
continues.

Humans, throughout time, continue to struggle with
what is the meaning of life and the purpose of man.
How often have you questioned your existence and the
reason for your being? Most will come to a place in life

and wonder, "What is the significance of man's individual contribution to the greater good of all?" Thus, leading to further questioning of the need for and the true existence of a greater being: What, if anything, did He purpose for "each" individual man? Think about it. How does one, in their human development and more importantly their spiritual development as sons and daughters of the King, begin to understand purpose, destiny, and fate? For one to begin this journey, I suggest it starts with a question, and that question is, "WHY?" It has been my experience that Christians are afraid to ask *WHY*—-believing that since God is sovereign and knows what He is doing, there is no room to question. This proposition, being no less true, does not hinder the believer from exploring and requesting an understanding of His way. Remember, in all thy getting, get an understanding.[3] I think we forget sometimes that He is able to provide us with an answer. Most often, He places these obstacles in our way to get us to a point of needing to communicate with Him through his divine design. It is up to us to know that He desires to commune with us, heart to heart. The issues of life are the discussions He is longing to have with His children.

---

[3]Proverbs 4:7 KJV

There is a point where we must arrive on our journey that will lead us to a safe place. In that safe place we are only then free to ask, *WHY?*

The quest in this endeavor then is, in some intelligible manner, to provide a sound biblical understanding of the "soul." I will explore how the scriptures help to create a uniform definition of this uncontainable substance that has, throughout history, provided controversy for many of the thinkers on the subject. After establishing the foundation for our discussion, we will elucidate on the scripture that declares... **"Even as the soul prospers"**[4] as to describe a developmental process that every individual must pass through to hear the truth of God declare He will withhold no good thing from you.

It is my intention to create a collection of ideas that will endeavor to declare the connection between personal growth and spiritual development, as well as to shape our understanding of God's desire for our life, his expectation for us to experience and to live the abundant life. Furthermore, my core belief is that

---

[4]John 1:2 KJV

personal growth cannot happen outside of spiritual growth; and the direct result of both will yield growth of the human soul. For these purposes, I define the human soul as the mind, the will and the heart contained inside the shell of flesh we know as the human body. I intend to separate the Christian practice from the true beauty of the Christian faith, opening the door to the powerful experience that awaits us once we are freed from the bondage of religious acts and rituals. This separation is an attempt to connect believers with the "universal soul" of the Christian believer. Thus, creating a connection with the belief in Christ the only begotten of the Father, Jehovah, the Creator God. It is this core belief that guides all Christian activity, however, the practice of this belief is played out in many different forms. It is the factors (i.e. race, socioeconomics, family, past experiences, hurts, successes, failures, etc...) which determine 'who and why' we are that influence our decision of how to practice our belief. Nevertheless, the truth remains that the core to each practice of the Christian faith is the central role of Jesus Christ. He is the anointed Son of God, who was born of an Immaculate Conception without sin to redeem lost man from their sins and reconcile them back to

God. I believe that when believers have this understanding as the thrust of their Christian journey all, other doctrinal issues take a back seat. Then the door opens to the understanding that God has a soul. His mind, will and heart is attempting to speak with each of the believers as He is preparing for Himself a body of believers equipped to rule and reign in the earth.

Finally, I will attempt to explain in my own words what the soul represents to me. Thus, opening the door for God to speak to you about His awesome ability to use our everyday life experiences to enrich us far beyond what natural riches could contribute to our lives. It is here that we will begin to hear God say, "Here is more; you have been faithful now receive the abundance."

Now let's construct the framework; the soul is the essence of all being and the driving force in providing human understanding of our existence. God breathed and man became a living soul. It is the "thing" that enables us to experience the aesthetic pleasures of life. The soul, as I understand it, is a complex substance; so complex and elusive that we as humans are often unable to recognize when the soul has been harmed, in a concept I have termed, "misalignment of the soul[5]." That which occurs when the soul of an individual has, as a result of some pain, tragedy, or hurt in life is lead on a path that is contrary to their true purpose and destiny. It is the occasion where individuals, as a result of confusion, travel a misguided path until someone adept in healing the soul assists in the realignment and refocusing process which includes the helping of the individual to tap into the purpose of God inside them and make use of it in the earth to bring God glory. This is the soul work this book will explore; connecting man to the purpose of God and the work of His spirit in the earth. Thus, the meaning of the soul is also intricately connected to one's understanding of the spirit of man. Yet, it is the comprehension of the difference between the two... soul and spirit ... that will yield greater understanding of what we believe God to be saying in the words "Even as the Soul Prospers." At the point when God divides the two, it is implied that the eternal work is completed in the spirit. He then re-engages the spirit into eternal covenant and the work of the soul enters into the process that must be walked out in our Christian experience in the earth. It is the soul that

---

[5]Hurt that changes the individual's direction or course of life. James Freeman

holds each of the memories, the hurt, the pains, the joys and even the traditions or what we in today's society have termed, "generational blessings and curses." As you commit to reading this book, know that God is beginning a process in you that will challenge you to evaluate your position about your past, your position in your natural family, and your emotional responses to each of these items moving forward. It is in this evaluation of your soul and spirit you will learn to declare, "It is not about me, the problems, the pains, the hurts, the good times or bad; it is about how God uses the situations He has designed for me in this life to get me to the place He prepared, that He might receive glory from my life." Can you hear Him? He wants to talk with you. Not just in your head, but from heart to heart. This is the communication we can experience from the development of the soul.

Another key point in the framework is the understanding that God created man in His image and in His likeness. This design is to provide insight into understanding one of the most important mysteries of God. It is often forgotten that we were created in His likeness and image to communicate with Him. Further, the difference in the creation of man and all the other creatures was that God, having completed all His other creations, wanted more than just another creature that would worship Him without cause. He desired our friendship. God continues this relationship of friendship with man by declaring that "His mercies are new every morning, His love never ceases..."[6] this is more than just the act of a savior; this is the act of a friend! Wow, the HUMAN was created to be the friend of the creator, GOD![7]

Additionally, there are several identifiable functions of the components of the soul. Consider the power of the mind and the heart to protect the human in trauma or traumatic life events from painful memories and events that are unable to be processed until a safe place is reached or created. There is also the ability of the body to use the mind and heart to heal itself and the ability to find internal peace in the midst of turmoil and chaos. It is this ability that continues to protect so many from the mental anguish of a break down and even the loss of control of the mind. The Christian must not forget that we are fearfully and wonderfully made. The wonder of

[6]Lamentations 3:23
[7]James 2:23

God's creation of man continues to be examined in many fields of the social sciences, as well as physical sciences, in an attempt to uncover the many different hidden secrets of this treasure. There have been several breakthroughs in research findings that support the role of prayer and meditation as a tool in the healing and prolonging of life after a "life threatening" diagnosis. Consider this; we are all born to die, but God, in His own way, awakens us to live. Through life in Christ, God has given man the opportunity to know Him and to declare that for the believers "It is all good." Therefore, when this trial is over, instead of being bitter I will be better, knowing that He does all things well! Our journey to prosper the soul now begins.

Quiet yourself. Listen, the voice of the Lord speaks to us softly as we endeavor to live in peace. It is not easy to determine not to live in the chaos of this life. The enemy has set the trap and waits for us to entangle ourselves in the yoke of the world's bondage. Don't! Remember, Christ declares our freedom from this world and seeks our entire focus. It is not beneficial for Christians to forget who they are in Christ. We are sons adopted and grafted into the plan of the Father to receive the inheritance of heirs. This is the prosperity that we seek, not just worldly riches for which we have no plan and no purpose. Ask yourself the questions: *do I see myself as a son? Am I operating in the rights and privileges associated with son-ship? Can others see this relationship in operation in my everyday life?* This is the life that Christ has designed for us. The ability to walk out His promises in the earth is our right. As I have developed in my personal relationship with Christ, more and more the focus shifts from material gain and possession, to more of Him. However, not knowing and recognizing at the time that I was declaring more of God...in that moment He was depositing in me His wisdom and developing in me the skills and competencies that attract natural wealth. I am constantly at a loss for words when I continue time and time again to listen to leadership gurus teach leadership as if it is something they have discovered a "new" truth; when in reality it is the truth Jesus spoke in the gospel or the instructions the Apostles left for us to follow as believers of the faith. I cannot be mad as these leadership thinkers are maximizing their moments. Take a moment and reflect what you hear God saying to you. I believe that those who commit to this exploration are seeking a fresh word from God about their individual situation. We are not often instructed to reach God for ourselves; we have preachers, prophets, and therapist; all of whom are good and have their place, but how many of us are after God? I want Him bad, and this book is a result of my earnest search. I am glad to report that I know a God who showed up!

Chapter 1

More than just a Savior... a Friend

Your Mercy

Your Mercy saw me
Right were I was
Standing in the need of A Savior
But most of all
In need of a Friend
Didn't let me enter the earth
Just to live and die
Didn't let me feel all this pain
Just to hear me cry…
Even though I was standing in the need of you
All I could see was my sin
So glad you looked pass my sin my need
And declared to me you're my friend
You're my friend…
Your Mercy Never ending
Your love never ceasing
New every morning…That's a friend

James T. Freeman
Copyright © 2005 by jtf95 Music

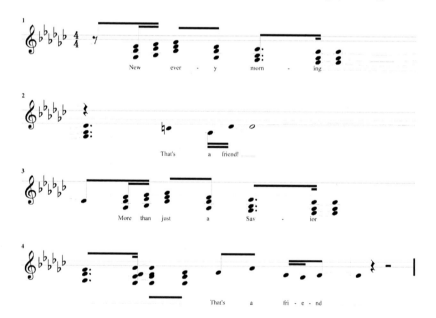

I t has become apparent to me through my experience in ministry that so often people attempt to reach the soul of an individual without first doing the groundwork. How can one expect someone to make choices about life and the hereafter, when one has not begun to make progression in his or her current state of being? I believe that one must first be introduced to him/herself so as to encourage a state of being that leads to a more in-depth understanding of self. Naturally or supernaturally what follows, is a greater understanding of the environment in which he/she lives in the "now existence." Human development teaches that individuals must reach a place of mastery in the current state before they can advance to the next level of development. This concept of development, explored in introduction to Psychology courses, can be viewed in several theories espoused by great thinkers such as Sigmund Freud, Carl Rogers, Piaget and Abraham Maslow. Each of these theorists suggests that the human species is more empowered when it is developing by building on the learning mastered in a previous stage of development.

Freud advances that the id, ego, and super ego are components of man developing through a continuum of experiences based on themes of self, family, safety, and sexual development. Rogers proposes that man develops through an actualization process of how he views himself through the eyes of others based on what he terms as "conditions of worth." Maslow contributes to the discussion on man's developmental process with the concept of the hierarchy of needs. He postulates that "basic needs" must be met before an individual can advance to his next level on the journey of life. All this to say that we are traveling on a journey, and to miss this point is to cripple the learning that needs to occur for movement and advancement to the next level. So often in life, I observe individuals who continue to experience the trials of life and when the trial is over; all they have is the experience of the trial. Again, I remind us that God is not in heaven playing a game with life. He is at work in us "to do His good pleasure."[8] He is working all things out for our good,[9] and is perfecting in us the things needed for operation in the kingdom of God. I urge you to find meaning in the things you encounter; your sufferings, your trials, your

---

[8]Philippians 2:13
[9]Romans 8:28

disappointments; whatever it is that you are going through, to allow God to speak to you through these events and experiences.

The American education history continues to instruct young American students (regardless of the nationality, ethnic or cultural background) that everyone has a right to life, liberty and the pursuit of happiness. Nevertheless, pose the question; *how can these grandiose ideals be achieved if the basic needs of a man constantly go unmet?* As a social worker, there is an important concept we share in the engagement and assessment process, as we assume the professional responsibility of ensuring that the population of the underserved is cared for in measure. This concept simply states that, "We must meet people where they are," but for this to occur the clinician must be equipped. Consequently, for this to occur in the kingdom of God, as it relates to the development of the human soul, we must understand the soul more. It has already been acknowledged from my viewpoint that the soul has eluded man and his understanding for some time. We have trivialized it, associated it with what we have a handle on and know as the spirit; we have associated it with the ethnic tradition of the African American culture (*i.e. soul food and soul music*). We have associated it with religion and salvation and much more, all in an attempt to understand it. Yet, we still struggle with what exactly this component of who we are is, and its purpose or what it was meant to accomplish in our lives on earth. Frightening, huh? The believer is forced to come to terms with his frailty; but is often encouraged to examine his god like quality. Catch the hint; the understanding of the soul begins the process for examining our likeness to God. Again, I must remind you that this is a road not often taken because of "fear." Even more disheartening, I suggest that one without this exploration will never truly experience the richness of the life that God has prepared for us in the earth. Child of God, there is a secret waiting for you when you dare to believe that He created you in His image and in the likeness of Himself. So, take the challenge He has for you. Declare with your words that which you seek, we are made in His image and likeness thus the creative ability is within us and waits for the redeemed to make declaration in the earth.

Now, this truth is hidden from you and waits for your development so that at the right time, you will walk into the revelation that God has been waiting on you and is anxious to perform your request. Can you hear Him? He is singing the sweet melody of, "Abide in me and my words abide in you...ask what *you will* and it shall be done."[10] This type of spiritual development pushes personal growth. How can one receive this powerful truth about oneself and not get closer to God?

The fact remains that we are all born into this life as sinners in need of a savior; but the relationship that God seeks is deeper than just supplying us a place of eternal rest in the after life. He clearly seeks to create an existence in this life that declares to the world, the angles, the enemy, and every principality that He is not only in control; He is in relationship with His creation. My experience as a clinician and worshipper has challenged me to seek clarity about the relationship of God to man. I have seen individuals in worship seeking answers, seeking peace, and simply looking earnestly for the deposit from God that will free them from the position of uncertainty to the position of knowing that

---

[10]St. John 15:7

they will successfully reach the next level. This same truth is discovered in the therapy session. People are looking for "peace." It is critical that Christians be able to answer the question "Is God able?" The answer must always be unequivocally *yes*. God can and will. However, the message must also be conveyed that God is more than just an answer to life questions or dilemmas. He is more than a rescuer. The sad truth is that many are walking this Christian experience beneath the rights and privileges available. We are not only the righteousness of God in the earth; we are a chosen generation, a royal priesthood,[11] who because of the relationship push pass the roles of servant and children to find friendship. Hear the words of the writer, "Friendship with Jesus fellowship divine..."

The mercy of God is so powerful. It looks beyond our insufficiency to our need, providing grace daily for the journey in such a way that His Mercy does not end, His love never ceases. Think about it, He is more than a savior. Superman represented a savior; the fireman a rescuer; your mom and dad might have saved the day with some thoughtful and unselfish deed; but the grace,

---

[11] 1Peter 2:9

mercy, and steadfast love of our God does more for us than any kind act.

Once we receive the revelation that God, the eternal and unlimited force of this universe is after more than just our salvation; it demands a response. He is presenting the opportunity to walk with Him, as did Enoch, Abraham, and Moses. This is the communion with the Eternal Spirit that produces life everlasting. It is a place of safety and peace; the position to know that as we walk with Him, He is pruning and showing us ourselves that we might be transformed by the renewing of our minds. This is the growth that leads to the position for the Christian to declare with the Spirit of God, *Even as the soul prospers!* It is in the growth of self-knowledge or, the growth of the mind, the will and the emotions as it relates to the individuals understanding and perspective of their role in this temporal existence in the earth, that God reveals to the believer Himself. The question still remains, *how do we reach people where they are if we cannot interpret where they are in their soul development?* It is critical that as believers we continue to spread the good news of the eternal life that can begin in *this* life. However, this message is limited to the receiver if they are not fully introduced to the love of God in the earth and its ability to perform more than just salvation. Once we hear the voice of God calling us to repentance, and we respond, we begin a walk with the Father that has many options. The first is the securing of eternal life. After the choice of eternal life, one must make the choice of abundant life in the earth. Inherit in this choice is the ability to walk in divine health, spirit, soul and body. Subsequently, we are then able to establish a foundation for the faith to enter the position of sons declaring with the Holy Scripture, *we are blessed and not cursed.* He gives us the wisdom to obtain wealth. Then declares to the believer, the wealth of the wicked is laid up for the just for our use in the kingdom.[12] At this point God's request is that we, with the sparrow, live in the certainty that our Father God is able, and will take care of all of our needs according to His riches in glory. For a moment, see the God that does more than saves; envision the God who is declaring, "I stand at the door, a gentleman knocking waiting for the invitation to come in and commune."[13] Not sacrificing His righteousness or his deity, He extends to us fellowship divine. That's a friend.

---

[12]Luke 12:32
[13]Revelation 3:20

Chapter 2

His Heart's Cry

His Heart's Cry

Looking back over my life
Trying to find the reason for so much strife
Why did it have to happen?
Why, did it have to happen?
Why did it have to happen to me?
If I could have just kept my head held high
And not always wondering the reason why
As I look up into the deep dark blue sky
I wondered if I would ever hear His heart cry
Jesus wants for you to hear
Jesus wants for you to wipe away the tear
Jesus wants for you to hear His heart's cry
That's what He wants
That's what He wants
That's what Jesus wants –Jesus wants for you to hear
His Heart's Cry
I want to know His heart's cry
I want to feel His heart's cry
To wipe the tear from His eye

James T. Freeman
Copyright © 2005 by jtf95 Music

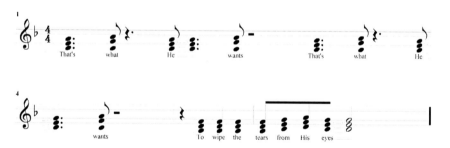

Thought: How can one *become*, if one has never learned to "be"?

For this writer, it is inherent in the stages of being (to be, to become, to have been) that one gains an increase in the understanding of self. Developing a keen sense of his likes and dislikes, an appreciation for the reasons these likes and dislikes exist, and discovering the meaning of life in relation to death and life.

Jesus said, "The whole law is summed up in the following saying that you must love your neighbor as your self."[14] It is my belief that inherent in this commandment was the instruction to get to know yourself before you begin to embrace, instruct or correct in Christian love. This commandment is an enormous task, but we often take for granted that we have somehow magically arrived at this point long before we actually truly reach attainment. There is a severe disconnect in the understanding of self in the modern age. As humans, we continue to observe the struggle for identity and self-awareness that is faced by many in their day-to-day exploration and on their

---

[14]Galatians 5:13-14 & Luke 10:27

journey toward self-definition. Examples are all around us; children and adults who struggle with sexual identity, individuals who lack the ability to interact socially and interpersonally with others, children and adults who as a result of family issues can not separate themselves from the issue and remain stuck in the inability to define themselves using the information gained from the family experience, and the list could go on. Therefore, this indicates indicating that all around us there are people who, for the lack of self-awareness and self identification, continue to flounder through life without purpose and suffer from an inability to experience the true soul changing power of God. It is at the point when we find our true selves that we can know God. There He speaks to us and makes us whole by declaring that all that you have gone through was designed specifically for you and will be used by Him to advance His divine purpose in your life. Wow, what a revelation! We can begin to see why God would say to us if one comes to this understanding, then they would be more able to complete the whole of the law. One would assume that an individual with this level of insight and revelation would be sensitive to the move of God in another person's life using the measure of grace and understanding that they have understood God to use in bringing them closer to Him. It has been postulated in the social sciences that when one is free to love and know him/herself that the ability to love and know others is much easier; thus there is a desire to come to know and love God. How then does one begin to grasp the concept of being? Is it simply grasped as one begins to understand ones self or is there something more? These questions and more provide for the initial journey of becoming; although, there may never be answers to the aforementioned questions.

We know that outside of the exploration of self, true development of the soul cannot occur. What we as Christian will continue to see, if we do not help people to tap into what God has called them and what He is attempting to do in their lives, are people who remain frustrated. These individuals are often mad with God and fearfully may never reach their designed potential in God. Their *"destiny"* if you will. It is a risk however; we must trust that God is able to do what He said He would do! What has been so discouraging, to so many Christians, is the unrealized dreams of those who have gone before us. Why is this? Is it because God was unable to perform or because others did not dare to believe? I would believe that so many who have gone before us came to Christ without knowing who they were and did not have strong sense of self or a love for their entire self that would have pushed an understanding that that which was in them was there for a purpose. It is my assumption that so many of our ancestors were running from who they were with the hope that Christ would make them "new," not understanding that from the beginning He foreknew and was using all of their life's experiences to establish His purpose in the earth.[15] I think back to the children of Israel who journeyed for 40 years. Why was this, we wonder? The Bible instructs us that the mindset of the people were not ready for what God had prepared for them and on several occasions, due to God's desire to give them the promise, they were unable to see in themselves what God was seeing. It is one of life's misfortunes that as humans one of our biggest barriers in life is the ability to see, know, love and accept ourselves for who God declares we are. It was at the point that Joshua and Caleb declared that they were well able to take the city[16]. We see God beginning to

---

[15]Romans 8:29
[16]Numbers 13:30

move, to set the stage for the possession of the promise. You may ask, "Why now and why does God declare that those who lingered in the wilderness could not go into the promise land?" Again, I would submit to you that until we know ourselves, we cannot "become" and until we "become," He will not come!

Faith without Works is Dead

As individuals, we often forget our participation in reaching the plan of God for our lives. Many of us believe that as a result of God's sovereign and omnipotent nature; He is going to do it all. Sorry, this is not the case. God provides us with what we need to accomplish the tasks He has called us to do in this life. We must know and believe all that is needed He's left inside of us. It is comparable to the three men in the parable of the talent. Each of the men was given the things they needed to begin their process according to their ability. Many of us, although we have been gifted and have the ability, may still not reach that place of prosperity of the soul due to fear and feelings of insecurity. This was true of the man who was given one talent. He was capable of maximizing the talent given to him; but not wanting to take the necessary risks needed to develop the gift that it might multiply, he hid it; giving back to the Master only what was given to him.[17] This, in my opinion, is one of the worst-case scenarios because most people desire to do their best and most feel pain when they feel unable to accomplish the task. Your fear is not an excuse!

It is often hard to hear God when He says to us that we have everything that we need working inside of us as a result of His strength that is in us. How often do we forget that Jesus makes the promise to us that He would not place upon us more than we can bear? This awesome promise is coupled with the comforting words that He, in His humanity, has felt each of the pains we feel; yet is saying to us *you must accomplish the work that you were sent to do.* Many times we, as humans, are hindered by the thought that maybe the task or the expectations are too unreasonable; here again is another opportunity where we experience amnesia. Recall that God in His foreknowledge predestined your work assignment and passed out the talents according to your individual ability. You have what it takes to complete that which God is impressing upon your

---

[17]Matthew 25:24-30

heart! Even after we have worked our way through all of the iterations, we still find ourselves doubting and unable to do what we know God has instructed. What is it at this point that blocks our soul and spirit from doing those things that are in us? For so many, the desire is strong, but there remains the hindrance of FEAR. This four-letter word gets in the core of our spirits and feeds as if it were food for the soul, which cause immobility. Much like the man with the one talent that hid it and returned it un-maximized to his master, fear will cause us to be deceived even from that which we know is true.[18] It will present lies to our soul and convince the mind that our immobility is in alignment with our purpose. In the name of Jesus we curse that lie! It is this type of food feeding the soul that continues to increase the great spirit of apathy, which holds us as Christians in bondage to not maximize the gifts and talents that God has given us. How then do we strengthen the soul? So that when the foods of fear and apathy attempt to enter the spirit to feed the soul, they are combated immediately. This is done by continuing to do self-assessments and by helping believers understand what is in them. So many times we forget or take for granted

---

[18] 1Corinthians 10:13

the role of our dreams in providing instruction to our purpose and destiny. Recall, it is *He* that is at work in us to will and do. Our dreams are often God's best opportunity to communicate with us. It is a time when our defenses are down and we are most vulnerable. Also, what are the consistent trials and tests in your life? These are often good indicators of what your purpose in ministry is and for whom God intends for you to minister.

I encourage each reader at this point to consider this thought: God is trying to speak to you. It is up to us to figure out what He is trying to say. We can accomplish this task by learning to be sensitive to His word and His will, the general will. Ask yourself this question, "What is God's plan for the earth?" How do you interpret God's interactions with Abraham when He was asked to go worship and use his only son, His promised seed, as the sacrificial offering? Now that we can see that God would have to give us His only begotten son as the ultimate sacrifice, consider for a moment, God asking Abraham to feel what He knew He would experience when Jesus would die upon the cross? Ponder this: if we are made in the image of our father, and we hurt and experience pain, and this most often is the source of our growth and development, what from his heart is he trying to get across to us his children? I want to know His heart's cry! We, in many instances, go in and out of our life circumstances and not really hear the word of God; He knows what He is doing. The scripture declares in Jeremiah 29:11 "He knows the thoughts he thinks `of me to bring me to a well thought out end."

Our father really knows what is best for us and seeks to communicate with us by allowing us to go through each life event and take from it a learning opportunity. It is this information that challenges us to see life in a new way and to understand and share with Him on new levels. It is extremely important that we do not frivolously go through life without understanding His purpose and will for each of the events presented for our experience. Bring back to mind that He has ordered our footsteps[19] and is seeking a certain result from each experience. So much so that after the test and trial, if the desired end is not met He sends you back through the test. See again the experience of the children of Israel; how they were in the wilderness for 40 years and this

---

[19]Psalm 37:23

was originally a 14-day journey. It was not until Joshua and Caleb were able to declare, even though there were giants in the land, "We are WELL ABLE!" It is the position of the believer to realize that the heavenly Father is waiting. God waits for us to see Him right and then He releases the right perspective for us to have of ourselves. It is only when we recognize Him and His strength that we can see our ability because we can only do all thing through Him.[20]

[20]Philippians 4:13

Chapter 3

Holding On To Your Promises

Don't Want To Die!

Holding on to His promises
Holding on to His word
Desperately in the hope to find the place of His rest (2x)
I don't want to die without knowing you in a real way
Die without knowing what I wanted to experience in this life that
you've given
For me to explore all the options and reasons
For the dreams and the visions you've birthed in my spirit
So I'll keep
Holding on to your promises
Holding on to your word
Desperately in the hope to find the place of your rest

James T. Freeman
Copyright © 2005 jtf95 Music

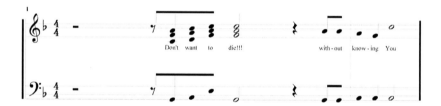

Don't want to die!!! with-out know-ing You

The Development of the Soul

The development of the soul continues to evolve over time. As individuals continue to experience life, the opportunity to understand that life is a process of seasons and cyclical learning is ever present, yet not always realized. One of the things that have come to light is that in the process of growth and development as humans, there are life lessons that are being offered, but it remains up to the individual to choose to embrace the learning process. Humans have been given a choice by God; we can continue in life being disgruntled, or we can decide to grow from each experience, disappointment, tragedy, and unexpected event that occur in our lives. The unfortunate reality is that these unexpected tragic life events, such as death, rape, murder or some other personal or family violation, are disappointing. They cause individuals to be thrown off from the place of peace promised by God. In addition, the individual's immediate response may result in intense feelings of being overwhelmed, yielding a response that focuses solely on themselves and how the event affected their life and expectations. It is this type of individual who lacks the ability, or the maturity in response, to see the opportunities inherent in the trials of life because they only see the disappointment of the event. Thus, it must be recognized that the process of choosing the learning moment versus the opportunity to emote or feel is not a natural or effortless choice. Humans will continue to struggle with the expectation that life is fair and "should" produce fair result for all. Consequently, the truth is that God is in control! He is infinite in His wisdom and understanding, and He typically chooses to use the struggles and difficult experiences we face as humans to reveal to us that He is in control. The Creator God says to us as His children, *in your weakness I am strong*[21]. This is usually very difficult for us to hear. We want harmony and we long for understanding. He says this way is revealed by faith and this way is a walk that will take trust in the fact that He is in control. Therefore, we labor to find this rest.[22] There remains a rest however one does not simply just walk up into the place of rest. It is the experiences of not understanding, yet trusting. It is the times when we could not comprehend, yet remain faithful and believe in His promise that He is in control. What an awesome God!

---

[21] 2 Corinthians 12:9
[22] Hebrews 4:9-12

How many times have we been in the midst of a situation and we began to wonder, "how God could allow this to happen" and "when is He going to end this trouble by rescuing, restoring and reimbursing me," for the unfair treatment we believed ourselves to have endured? Nevertheless, He waits for us to come to the knowledge that He is all knowing; nothing happens by chance and there are no coincidences in our walk with Him. One would think that we as Christians, being empowered with this revelation, would find ourselves in control and willing to walk through each of our trials with the confidence and faith that we win. Consequently, the walk of the Christian continues to be weakened by the inability to see ourselves as God sees us. We continue to examine our faults, wonder if we are on the right path, wonder if we made the right choice, or if God is displeased because we continue to fall. We, who should be the praise of His glory[23], continue to lose time pondering if His wisdom accounted for our insufficiency. There is hope! Never forget that this is a set-up, those who believe are declared the winners. God has chosen to use our pain for our development, and when we allow Him to do so,

---

[23]Ephesians 1:12

there is a growth in the inward part of us that far outweighs the pain. Recall our light affliction is but for a moment, it works in us a far more exceeding and eternal weight of glory.[24]

The soul is in a process, it is now developing in stages. The question then becomes, *at what stage does the process start?* This writer argues that long before one receives the miracle of salvation that the process has begun. It is more than receiving the learning that all things work together for the good.[25] It is the ability to undergo intense disappointment, yet see the hand of God moving. It is moving from the place of emotional immaturity to a place where we face God as mature beings with the knowledge that He is in control. We propose that the soul develops in the following manner:

- **Phase One, Emotional Immaturity:** The self consumed understanding and child like emotional response to suffering, problems, loss, and disappointing events. It is in this phase that the soul is emerging. The individual is beginning to recognize or become conscious that there is some greater force of

---

[24]2 Corinthians 14:17
[25]Romans 8:28

existence that lies at the core of his being that is shaping. This force is yearning for the opportunity to have an impact on the emotional response to life events. It is here that believers recognize the internal struggle that exist to return some portion of the creation of man back to the Creator. I suggest that in each human God has placed a longing in the heart for a God who will make sense of their life. Consequently, we find individuals on this journey of life who, in their response to life, attempt to determine the fairness or sensibility of a creator who declares he is all powerful, just and in control of all life events. This stage of the development is always in existence; however it waits for the individual to awaken to the need for their contribution to the growth process of this force that is in existence within them. It is like the flow of electricity within a house that waits for a force to turn on the light or plug in a socket; God is at work in us waiting for us to come alive to this truth. Enter into the operation of this truth. I declare that the revelation of this truth will change your understanding of everything you experience in this existence. It is time for movement in the body of Christian believers. God desires to see manifestation in the earth and to see those who are born again to the Christian faith mature. The growth He desires is the advancement of the believer's awareness and ability of their position as children of God in the earth; not only in their ability to build churches and denominations but to build the believer's emotional responses of the soul.

- **Phase Two, Emotional Enlightenment:** The ability to acknowledge that suffering, problems and disappointments hurt, but maintain the position and faith that God is in control. In this phase, the soul is being shaped. The individual recognizes the soul and understands the process that God is using. He uses life events to impart knowledge and communicate with man. It is in this phase that one can say, "Lord, I know that you are in control, but I cannot see what you are doing in my life, but I will have faith that you are God!" Much like all other developmental theories, in this phase we see the childlike immaturity turn to adolescent curiosity. The believer in this phase declares in the mind a belief in the greater good and purposes of God. Then he strengthens the will to pursue the determined choice of the mind while struggling with the emotional dilemmas of the heart in response to information received from varied life events. The believer, in this phase, is testing the information learned in the previous stage. In the previous stage, the believer learns there is a force inside, desiring to reconnect with the Father God, which uses life events to grow within the believer, strengthening them for their work in the earth realm. God has a plan that prepares the collective body of believers to complete the work He has begun in the earth. The believer now has information that helps to place emotional responses in perspective. It is with this perspective that the individual is empowered to move the agenda of God, to its rightful position. This growth process of the soul permits the believer's interpretation of life events to take on meaning and be used for the spirit. It is this reconnection to the purpose of God for His creation that peaks the individuals curiosity to exercise the truths of God's word. It is here you will see believers declare with the scripture, "I can do all things through Christ..." and begin to ask their circumstance, *is there anything too hard for God?* I believe that the information the believer receives in the first stage pushes them to tap into their inner God likeness. Although the glimpse of God-likeness is very immature and is still developing, there is an awareness of something more that arises within, that strengthens the ability to keep holding on to the promises. In this inner position we can observe the soul enlarging in shape and strength, gaining new information, exploring new challenges and applying the new truths it receives in the process. If this is your phase, whisper to God this prayer: *The pain still hurts yet I believe. I feel the push to hold on, I receive every promise in your word that declares that I am your heir in the earth, that I have the rights and privileges as I have been adopted fully into the family of father God. I accept the assignment to observe to do all that Jesus, your example for sons in the earth, has established as the protocol to expand the kingdom. I declare that I am a kingdom citizen; this world is not my home. I am seated in heavenly places, and my desires are not on the things of this earth. In the strength of this understanding, I accept the charge to rule and have dominion. I declare, to every circumstance that comes my way, I will see the salvation of the living God knowing that he is in control and is using every situation to reveal to me something about His ability and my role in the earth. I inform every plan of the wicked one that I will not die without knowing, I will live and fulfill every promise He prepared for me. I will see the word of God come to pass in my life to His glory and honor. Amen.*

- **Phase Three, Emotional Awakening:** The ability to experience suffering, problems, and disappointments while knowing that God is up to something. In this phase, the soul is prospering. It has emerged and has been shaped, and is now growing—- moving from one glory to another. In this phase, the individual declares," He that has begun a good work in me shall perform it.[26]" There is, in this phase of the soul's development, a certain trust that comes to the surface; unlike in the first two phases in which the belief develops and is put into action. It is here you will see the believer take a stand in confidence that though He slay me, I trust Him.[27] The believer in this phase actualizes the word of God in their everyday life. This individual arrives at a place in their emotional response that declares, *I just cannot give up.* It is the looming notation that *there is something more,* the belief that God is using what I am going through and I am persuaded to see the end. I believe in this phase, the individual learns to use his or her emotional responses as a declaration of their maturity in the things of God. It is here you will see that the individual responsibility the

---

[26]Philippians 1:6
[27]Job 13:15

believer assumes is unlike the emotional responses exhibited in any of the other two phases. Here, as a result of the emotional awakening, the believer developments a trust in the divine will and purpose of God that gives shape to the soul and provides the necessary strength for growth and future development. It is this awakening that now changes the existence of the believer on his Christian walk. The walk is no longer solely about the after life; eternal life begins while here on the earth in this realm. It is the learning of how God seeks to use our responses in the earth to reveal truth to us that will enlarge the scope of our understanding of His universal truth that will last an eternity. Consider this; God is challenging each believer to live in eternity now. This truth will change your existence, causing you to move from the position that I am living my life to ensure that on that great day of judgment, my faith will be in the position that I will be availed the opportunity to enter into His heavenly kingdom. I declare, live now!

Embrace the truth. At creation, God in His foreknowledge seen you afar off. Your ability to hear and respond to the call of God settles the issue of your eternal peace. I wish I could explain it in a way where everyone can put to rest the struggle of what the after life will present however, some things God reserves for Himself and instructs us to trust. Welcome to the journey where we dare to get close to our God. If you are still reading this, I know you hear Him calling you close. Draw nigh; He will draw nigh to you at your response to the call.

Fear not, these phases do not occur over night. God patiently waits for us to come into the full knowledge of Him. I am reminded of the story of Job. It was after Job had gone through the developing test that built his faith that God said to the enemy, "Have you considered my servant Job?[28]" We must remember that God is using our lives as testimonies and often that which we are going through, is not just for our own growth but also for the growth of the body of Christ. How many times what you have gone through blessed your neighbor and

---

[28]Job 1:8

as a result of knowing someone who has stood the test of time, you have been strengthened in your test? The Old Testament declares that iron sharpens iron[29] and the New Testament instructs us to bear the burdens of the weak. There is a school of thought that I have been introduced to in my Christian experience that declares interpersonal relationships are tools in which God uses to heal our wounded souls. As Christian journeymen, we tend to look for the things that we believe God is speaking as it relates to us as individuals, and miss the powerful opportunity to experience God as we relate to our brother or sister as *it* relates to our shared human experience. As an individual who has grown up in the church and has been trained to identify my Christian experience with religious activity, it has been tremendously hard to accept that God has limited His interaction with me to my ability to interact with my brother or sister in this shared human experience. Wow, at the point that God began to open this concept up to me through the teachings of Apostle Gerald Loyd, I immediately resisted this truth. How could the Creator God, who is dynamic and personal with any human who opens the door and allows Him in, require that our

[29]Proverbs 27:17

fellowship with each other in the earth determine the level to which our relationship with Him advances? I quickly began to run through all of my former teaching and the things that I had come to understand... God is personal; He is Love; He will be there when everyone else forsakes you; He is your friend when you're lonely. This to me sounds like a God who is there for you when nothing else is going right. I thought surely God would never limit His interactions with us by our interactions with each other. Nevertheless, I continued to listen in my spiritual ear, as my natural ear and my flesh resisted and stood up in defiance. I was fearful at the thought of my relationship with God depending on my ability to build relationships with others, as this was an area I had not been completely successful in times past. I began to hear and to comprehend that God, in challenging the believer to fellowship and love each other, was trying to impart a piece of Himself in His children. I started to return to my basic understanding of the existence of man. God wanted someone to commune and fellowship with; a being that would share His dominion, the ability to rule, to subdue and to replenish, thus He created an image, and then He made man. As difficult as it was, I took the plunge to receive the lesson; could it possibly be that God was trying to instill in me, as one of His sons, the empathy and love that He employed when He created man in His image? To love Him we must first love each other. Reluctantly, I traveled on this road in the attempt to discover what God intended to reveal.

Can you imagine a life without challenges or an individual who is unwilling to be molded to new ways of thinking? This individual, or state of being that refuses growth, is stagnant and will ultimately lead to death. The Father patiently waits for the believer to enter into the rest He has prepared for us. I believe there is a hidden truth that God anxiously waits for the body of believers to embrace. This truth is that together, we are a force against the plan of the wicked that can not be stop. It is no surprise that the enemy works so hard to bring the spirit of contention and sowing seeds of discord among the body of believers. The earth, the enemy, and all of creation knows that once the body of believers embrace their role in the kingdom, there will be birthed an order that can not be challenged, nothing will be impossible to us as we embrace the authority for mature sons of God. It is critical that the body receives this truth. The growth and development of the soul is the key to the next move in the kingdom. God desires knowledgeable children in the earth who are fully developed. The promises are prepared for us, yet He waits for us to embrace purpose, and for our words, actions and faiths to mature to take the kingdom by force.

I've often wondered, what keeps people from experiencing a full existence in this life? For so many people, living means being able to have and do some of the thing that are often denied or appear unattainable. Consider this; how many of the individuals that live in poverty can focus on the concept of, "saving?" If one came to preach prosperity to the poor, even though "savings" is an integral part of understanding the movement from poverty to prosperity, it would be a roadblock for those individuals because in their mind (a component of their soul) they do not have money to save; they are just barely surviving. I ask then, "Is it impossible to preach prosperity to the poor in that their minds are consumed with their state as being in poverty/poor (assuming that this state is universal to all poor)?" Of course, movement is possible, but only once one begins to understand that it is not the movement of the individual from poverty to prosperity, but the movement of the soul!

The loss of dreams produces the loss of hope...

In the process of life and interaction with others, I have observed the scary reality of when people loss hope and cease from striving for the fulfillment of their dreams. This interaction has lead to the question, "why does this occur?" What happens that makes people lose hope in the ability of their dreams coming true? Let's imagine how one must feel about God when this occurs. I once heard a minister recant, "People lose hope and express anger not because they don't believe God is able, but because they know He is able and become increasingly mad when they are forced to interpret 'why if you are able you have not moved on my behalf.' In my prayer time, God has reminded me that there is an appointed time; a due season. And He is constantly encouraging us not to lose hope. He says to us, *do not be weary in well doing you'll reap if you faint not.*[30] We must be willing to hold on to our faith in the midst of bad situations and trust that since God said it, He *will*

---

[30]Galatians 6:9 & 2 Thessalonians 3:13

perform it! This becomes hard when things do not occur within the span of our time limits. What then is God getting at? What is being birthed in us? Could it be that faith, hope and love are the fruits of the components of the soul? This line of questioning and the process of life have taught me that in order for God to prosper and grow the soul, He begins by strengthen the components. Once the components are strengthened, they begin to bear fruit. God renews the mind with His word, thus changing the very thought patterns and expectations. It is then that God starts to activate the fruit faith as a result of ones hearing the word. Then He gives us the desired part of Him; His love. He says to us, "without faith it is impossible to please me."[31] Once you have faith, the challenge is hope; the determination not to give up on that which has been promised or believed. This is the fruit of the will, that ability to locate the place within the mind that declares a position and assembles all your strength to stand firm in hope. For we are saved by hope, but hope that is seen is not hope; for what a man sees, why doth he yet hope? But if we hope for that we see not, then do we with patience wait for it.[32]

---

[31] Hebrews 11:6
[32] Roman 8:24-25

Therefore, after hope has been established, He reminds us that the most important of the triad is love. What kind of love is God talking about? I believe it to be the love of God that never ends, the love that consistently seeks the good of the believer, and the love that is renewed daily. It is this love that releases the soul of man to discover the strength necessary to prosper and to grasp hold of the promises of God.

How do we keep from losing hope in our dreams? What are the practical ways of maintaining in the face of the reality that God operates in His timing and not ours? In today's society, it has become so easy for individuals to lose faith and hope. We see so much poverty, abandonment, and loss, which lead us to wonder "why?" It is so hard, but we must STOP feeling sorry and begin to bring *meaning to our suffering*. It is suffering that causes awareness of the issues of the soul. The process of not abandoning hope in our dreams is not easy. I believe that God knows that our faith will be challenge; but encourages the believer to know in their 'knower' (the soul if you will) that what we believe or dream for is our purpose in Him. Know that God is responsible to bring it to pass and it will ultimately bring

Him glory. This is the challenge for the believer, it is a process to locate the dream that God has hidden in you for you to give it back to Him for His glory. Once the dream has been identified it is our job to now familiarize ourselves with the promises of God in the word. It is at challenging times, when it would seem easiest to give up, you can declare with the word *I am holding on to His promises.*

We as humans get so angry at suffering, but we fail to understand that it is our pain that helps us get to some of our best days. I am not sure how to help one keep from losing hope from time to time, but I will encourage one not to give up hope. We must remind ourselves that as children of the king of kings. He has not forgotten us. Tell your circumstances that it is not our responsibility to make our dreams a reality; it is He who has predestined us[33] after He foreknew our destinies. Remember, our destiny is not a matter of chance but of choice;[34] we cannot give up now, we are so close to receiving the harvest God has established for us before time began.

---

[33]Romans 8:29
[34]William Jennings Bryan

Chapter 4

Can't Give Up

Can't Give Up

I just can't give up believing on Him
I just can't give up believing on Him
He is my everything
He is my All in all
I just can't give up believing on Him
Even in my trouble times
When it gets to hard to bear
Dark clouds won't go away
My blue sky has now turned gray
Can't get the sun to shine
No peace within my mind
Feeling like I lost my grip
Trying hard just not to slip
I just can't give up believing on Him

James Freeman

Finding One's Soul by Understanding the
Past via Receiving

The wisdom of those who have gone before us

For many of us, we get confused and tangled up in the web that our forefathers (our moms, dads, grandmas, and grandfathers etc…) have left for us. Some of those things we are thankful for, some of the other things hold us back and keep us bound to numerous thoughts, ideals, concepts, ways of life, customs and rituals. Why is this so? Each of us at some point, has declared about the discipline and the rules of our parent, "I am NEVER going to be like my parents," but what happens? It is inevitable; we are mirrors of them at some level. There are forces at work beyond our control, and no matter how hard we try to escape, we belong to their legacy. As a piece of that legacy, we live and pass it on in the lives of our offspring. In psychology, we learn that some mental illnesses are termed hereditary. This indicates that if, something occurred in the mother or father it is most likely (highly possible) to occur in the child. My question is *what really causes the correlation*? Does the faulty thinking and fears of being like a parent have an effect? Or can it be possible that we unknowingly create what we have seen as a result of our fears and expectation about life? The nature/nurture debate of psychology suggests that there are certain innate characteristic that are imprinted on each individual as a result of the biological make up. Thus, even if the individual did not know or was not raised with their biological family, these imprints would chart behaviors and experiences that would be similar to that of other members who share the same biological make up. The other side to the debate is that behavior is learned as a result of the certain types of environments the individual experiences, such that a violent child regardless of the biological make up, as a result of the violence in the home produces violence in the individual's behavior. I believe there is truth to each side of the debate and neither bares more truth than the other; however, could it be there is yet another realm of being in operation? I suggest there is also the realm of the growing soul. Up to now we have understood life as an attempt to demonstrate that people are in process to maximize his/her potential. I know life is a lot of hard work and the road called "easy street" does not exist. Whether one is living in poverty or wealth, believe it or not, the issues do not change, they simply look different. Each, when faced with the opportunity to hear the call of God, must make a choice to respond. The earthly possession can, and will not assist in answering the call. It is that which is on the inside of man that will stand to respond to this great challenge. I suggest that in our quest of Christian understanding, the depth of one's Christian walk can be passed to their future generation. The experiences and relationships that I have built with God cannot be deeded to my children; but once they tap into the call for themselves, the revelation and information obtained in my walk with God is a foundation for them to build upon.

So how does putting together the pieces of one's past help them in developing the soul? This question is answered by several factors.

1. **Walking in the Family Purpose:** The forefathers have paved the way for you. This means some of the troubles, trails and tribulations they have experienced, you don't have to repeat. Their success cleared a way for you to take the family vision farther and do much more to advance the legacy for the next generation. The deposits

they leave in your account allow you the opportunity to develop your soul faster and pass it on even more valuable for the next generation.

2. **Uncovering the unrevealed family truth:** There is also information that has been concealed or hidden that blocks progress. These situations are demonstrated in repeating cycles. In my experiences they are seen in family issues of sexual abuse, teen pregnancy, or mental illnesses (like depression and over eating). Individuals are constantly striving to overcome these obstacles, not recognizing that until in some manner they are able to close the door on the family issue with the help of God, their soul is in bondage to that issue. In effort to be fair to the truth of this revelation, it is not always a negative behavior that is being uncovered. There are individuals who have had much potential, and for whatever the reason, (fear, insecurity, unbelief) did not maximize. The task of the next generation is the contention with the struggle to

uncover the family vision, the reason it did not grow and the ability to stop the cycle.

Take heart. Hear the word of the Lord that declares, *take my yoke upon you, the authority is given to the son by the father, and learn of me for my yoke is easy and my burden is light thus you will find rest for your soul.*[35] It cannot be forgotten; God is using our experiences to get us to the point where we discover that there is no other help but Him.

Finally, when we arrive at the point that we desire Him more than anything else, we receive the eternal truth that He alone is the source of strength and in the midst of the most difficult trial we declare, *I just cannot give up.* This understanding forms the foundation for future growth and understanding, not the position of our family members in the earth. God uses them, but in relation to what He is doing in our lives, the role of our natural family does not compare. The power now lies within each individual to determine to use all of life events, past hurts, successes, and future aspirations to determine that my life belongs to God and it is to be

[35]Matthew 11:27-30

used to bring Him glory. I believe that this truth will free the believer to dare to dream big. Dreams, in my opinion, are the tools that God uses to take us from one position in life to the next. In my experience, my dreams—-under the inspiration of the Holy Ghost—- were the vehicles that provided the push needed to gather the strength necessary for the journey...even in troubled times!

This chapter is titled *'Can't Give Up'*. It encourages the reader to understand the position held for every believer must reflect a determination to finish. Consider the commitment God makes with the believer to complete His work in us[36]. We must commit to our position in Him that is secure in the heaven. As I have endeavored to complete this chapter, I considered many of the difficult things I have experienced in this life. It has been my experience that I tend to forget most of the scenes that would replay in my head. A protective measure of the mind, in that the mind will lock away unwanted or traumatic memories that the individual is unable to process, for which I am grateful. There is a place in the unconscious mind of each individual that

---

[36]Philippians 1:6

houses memories the individual is not in the position to confront healthily.

I have always, to my recollection and stories told to me by my elders', been a "dreamer," living in a world created and occupied by me. This has made it difficult for me to distinguish the dream from reality. At the tender age of five, I was introduced to a concept that would change the course of my life. I was sexually abused. I was prematurely exposed to information that should have been protected from me. I have learned from this experience, if unstopped by spiritual truth and emotional healing, it is inevitable that the sins of the generation before will seep into the next. Can you hear Him? He is declaring that the power to stop the cycle is in the earth for us *now*. Do you want to be a part of the generation that purges the family line, helps to bring the clarity of God to the family purpose and causes the members who are in bondage to walk free? This is the power we have as believers. It is more than a dance in the assembly. There is power that belongs to us in this hour that is longing to show forth the demonstration of our father in the earth. My abuse experience occurred with in my family, and as was expected, "the system" ran to my rescue. Never confronting the hurt, the pain or the shame that accompanied the experience, the event was fixed and declared wrong and was never to occur again. Thank God it did not, but the scar that was left coupled with the viewpoint I was now attempting to interpret life, made my growth process that much more difficult. It is here that I have seen God declare that no matter what the experience, I will use it for my glory. There is no experience that you will face in this life God is not familiar with and will be challenging you to move forward no matter what the challenge or issue. Many will declare that if raped, abused, molested, or left to grieve the loss of a family member who died tragically, that the individual will face a challenge in moving forward from this event. I am sent here to challenge this lie. Our God has given us the promise that we are to have peace if we keep our mind on Him. We can, with the lily of the field and the sparrow, know that God is our Father and will provide all of our needs. In this position, we can now make up in our minds that, *I will be anxious about nothing.* It does not matter what the situation is. If we are in Him, then the things we experience will bring Him glory. Stand up, take your position. There is a position for the believer in the earth no matter what life has served you that position is to use it all to bring Him glory in the earth. Receive the assignment. Declare it again, *I can't give up.* Can you see it? God is waiting for us to set our affection on things above; there is nothing in this earth that should separate us from His love or our ability to return love to Him. Know this there; is now NO condemnation. I encourage each reader to determine within themselves that, *"God wanted me."* This is the only way to hear the call and be strengthened to response. Again, I state what the scripture declares; it is not by our might or strength but by His spirit.

We all at some point declare about the rules set by our parent(s); some of their habits, laugh, dress, etc., "I am NEVER going to be like my parents." Believe it or not, and I reiterate, there are forces at work beyond our control. We belong to their legacy, and a piece of this legacy *we* live and then pass on in the lives of our offspring. Consequently, this truth must push each believer to search the history of their individual family and become familiar with the family patterns and cycles as to avoid pitfalls and future perpetuation of unnecessary family issues that keep individuals from maximizing in this life and preparing/positioning the next generation. Salvation for the believer does not remove you from your family or its history. The position of the believer is made more potent if the understanding of your family history and God's purpose for it is revealed to you as you walk out your purpose in the earth.[37] The misfortune of most traumatic family events is that no one ever wants to own up to the truth or to search out the why God would allow the event to occur to them or within their family. As a result, the members participate in the creation of masks and other defense mechanisms that shield us; allowing us to take the position to, "NEVER let anyone see you sweat." It is time for us to remove the mask and be strong enough in our faith, and in God, to examine the truth of our history, if what we believe to be true is "truth." We must receive the word that there is no thing that occurs without purpose. So be strengthened in your faith and seek the Lord's will for your individual life. Just as Jacob decided, do not let go until you get the blessing that changes your name and makes your journey in this life make sense.

---

[37] Isaiah 51:1

I grew up in a family where strength was honored and expected, you were taught to be a survivor. Therefore, when I never found the answers to the many times I have asked the question "why me", I began to ask different questions; "God, what now? What are you trying to teach me now?" It was here I began the journey to make sense out of what was going on in my life and the lives of those around me. I quickly learned that God uses our lives to reveal to us His truth. This truth then challenges us to use the revealed information to help others in their journey to bring Him glory in the earth. We are building a kingdom. *Lord, let your kingdom come, let your will be done in the earth as it is in heaven.* Are you ready? In reading this book, you are declaring to your circumstances and experiences you have gone through that *I will not be bound any longer to challenges of my journey. Declare it… I will let nothing separate me, NOTHING!* Listen, I hear him in this moment saying pick up your bed and walk. I encourage each reader to consider this; God wants you more than you want Him. *His desire for you is so deep that He sacrifices the life of His son Jesus to experience you through this sacrificed life, and when He see you, He see you as a being without sin.*

Once we receive this truth, the challenge is to determine if the spirit is reconnected and eternal life begins at the point we answer the call from God, with the heart making confession with the mouth, what to do next. I have written this book because I believe that we enter a walk with God that takes each believer on a journey inward that will develop the soul. It is this understanding that has caused me to examine the wealth I have received from the family God has assigned me to by the order of my blood birth. The gift that I received from being a member of such a loving, caring, protecting and giving body of people has been priceless. It is this type of nurturing that has caressed this dreamer and the desire to discover meaning in this existence (or better termed, *the soul*). My motivation resulted from the circumstances, conditions, customs and caress of my family. I have watched some powerful people come and go; passing through this life without ever reaching what I perceive could have been their fullest potential; dying, in my opinion, premature deaths yet passing on the hope to their young to do better, to be more. I still ask myself today, what is it that kept them (my forefathers and mothers) from maximizing? The concept of history is untold yet relived so many times in us (the offspring) everyday as the cycle continues unbroken. I have made sense of the pain; the many questions of, 'why.' The answer is, because freedom MUST come! FREEDOM for Robert, Raymond, Daniesha, Taniesha, Leon, Scott, Thomas, Akuila, Davon, Lakiesha, Levelle, Derrique, Khayla, Dajah, Tiona, Kendra, Jalah, Joshua, George, Andre, Madison, Yvonne, Honesti, Raeonah and Raymond …. I accept the assignment and recognize that it is my duty to ensure the release of the next generation from the pain of the past. I must tell them that as creations of God we are more than average. It is God's plan and documented in His word that we are MORE than![38] I must encourage them to dream so that they may learn that it is our dreams that God chooses to make our reality. Thus, reminding them always that it is God's good pleasure to give to His children the Kingdom.[39] And always keeping them conscience of the fact that God says to us, "Eye have not seen, neither have ears heard or has it even entered into the heart of man what good things God has in store for us."[40] Never allowing them to forget that the God we serve declares, "I will do

---

[38]Romans 8:37
[39]Luke 12:32
[40]Isaiah 64:6 & 1 Corinthians 2:9

exceedingly abundantly above what you ask or think...".[41] God is waiting for your dream, so dream as if your life depends on it, because it does!

---

[41] Ephesians 3:20

Chapter 5

The Place of Rest

The Place of "Rest"

He prepares a table before me
In the presence of my enemy
He requires of me to sit and eat
When all around me there's no relief
He anoints my head with oil
My cup runs over
Surely He Shall...
Even though I walk through the valley where death cast a shadow
Surely He Shall...
I will fear NO evil for thou art ever present and with me
Surely He Shall...
Thy rod thy staff shall comfort guide protect and keep me
Surely He shall...
That's why I'll always declare
The place of rest
See it
Believe it
Receive it
Even if your:
Standing in the midst of the fire
Swimming in the midst of the flood
Learning in the midst of my trial
Trust in the power of the Lord

Psalm 23

The Place of Rest

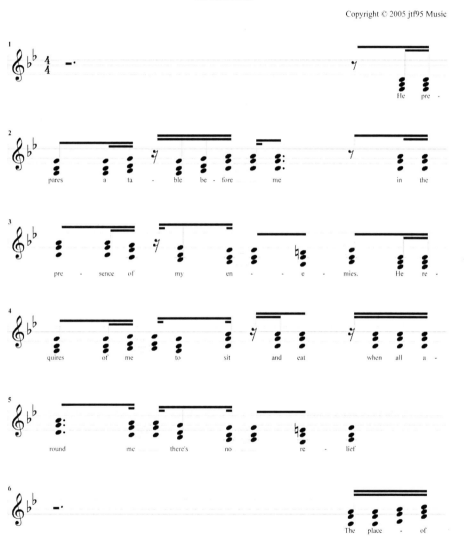

What in your life experience is God using to tell you who He is and how He feels?

Knowing that He is a God who does nothing by chance, and knowing that He knows the end from the beginning, what is He saying and how can we stay tuned? Lamentation 3 reminds us that God takes no pleasure in our pain.[42] Now we have determined, no matter what life sends our way, not to give up. The opportunity is left for us to discover if this (whatever the event is) has occurred, what can I do with the information and how can it bring God glory. I will admit; losing focus is so easy. Often in our experience we find ourselves searching for dreams. It is in our inability to understand how to make those dreams reality that we become frustrated and discouraged. Nevertheless, we must continue to labor and work to maximize the purpose of God for our life in the earth. So, don't get disheartened at failure and begin to question the efficacy of dreams. It is His will that we prosper. This is a trick of the enemy to rob you of your heritage in the kingdom. Never forget, God waits for us to find our place in Him and tell the enemy, and any

---

[42]Lamentation 3:21-26

situation that is experienced in this life, that it will not keep us from bringing Him glory. We can trust in the hope that the dream will come true. Make up in your mind even now; let the enemy know that you know it was never about you, but you recognize the call of God and submit to His purpose. It is in this position that we can assume the position of rest knowing that God will not deny Himself. That which He has put in us will come to pass. The truth is simply that it is not a complicated task to experience the loss of hope, as we have discussed in the last chapter. Nevertheless, many times I've questioned God saying, "why is this," and "if it is your will for us, then why the struggle to hold on?" Yet we declare with the Psalm of David that the Lord is my Shepard and I shall not want.

As we continue to journey through life, we discover that life is a mystery, which is most often revealed by simple acts in nature. God reminds us often that His ways are not our ways nor does His thought correspond with ours.[43] Attempting to employ our wisdom to uncover the secrets of His will leaves man confused. I'm reminded of the story on Nebuchadnezzar (King of

[43]Isaiah 55:7-11

Babylon) and how he, being one of the most powerful kings, became caught up in himself, thinking himself to be bigger than he ought to, and was brought down by God. He was struck with the spirit of insanity, roamed the dessert for years, hair was never cut, and his nails grew long. It took all of this for a king to declare, *there is no other God outside of the ancient of days, the King of Glory, the Jehovah God.*[44] As Christians we tend to forget the promise that we are the praise of His glory. God is in covenant with us. We cannot afford to loose hope or to allow our faith to waiver. As we draw closer to the age of His return, it becomes more important for us to be able to demonstrate the power of belief in His word.

Don't forget, God has a plan... He desires to prosper you. Not only the prosperity of the soul. God seeks first to restore the person. His desire is for the character—-the inner you—-to be restored to right relationship with Him. Once this relationship is restored, He begins to speak freely to your spirit reminding you that it is He who will give the wisdom to get wealth.[45] This relationship (the healing of the soul) is the force to a

[44]Daniel 4:33-34, & 37
[45]Deuteronomy 8:18

greater walk with God. It is here that we learn to trust His word!

I often say a babe in Christ is a precious commodity. Over time, I have watched God rush to care for babes in the faith, simply to prove to them He is able. He hastens to fulfill His word for them in an effort to build their faith and trust in Him. This is an exciting process to observe. The growth of the soul (that inner part) that had been cut off from God as a result of a sin we did not commit. Take this opportunity to ponder the truth of the statement, "This journey is not about the believer, we are here for His pleasure." It is not personal, just a simple reminder *it is not by strength nor by power but by His spirit.*[46]

God is gracious. He continues to chide with man, (He is so patient) allowing us to mature and become the men and women that He calls forth from the state we find ourselves in before He speaks. It is difficult for us to totally comprehend the goodness of God due to our inability to participate in thoughts on His level. Thus, it calls for the constant reminder that we are in His plan.

---

[46]Zechariah 4:6

He is God; He does not make any mistakes and nothing happens by chance. It is our duty to remind, and be reminded, that predestination occurred after His "forethought." He foreknew everything that was to occur prior to His design. So how can we learn from these occurrences? We as individuals can begin to remind ourselves that God is in control! He is NEVER allowing life to happen to us more than He is challenging us to rise to another level of faith and declare our faith and trust in His ability to be God. This means that at the point when it seems hopeless, unfair, and unjust, we must be reminded that due to the relationship God has called us to as being one of His sons, the victory is already in our possession. He is in control. Hear again, the Lord speaks to us from His word with instructions to rest. There is a place in Him that will cause your spirit to be at peace and find the place where we can, with the word of God, be anxious for nothing but with everything by prayer and supplication make our request known to God.[47] How powerful to be in a place where when we pray, we believe that it is done. Even when we do not see the earthly manifestation there is a trust and faith in the

---

[47]Philippians 4:6

promise that God is in control and is working all things together for the good. This still does not account for the pain that is experienced while one goes through the test. Once, I recall asking God,"Why, if you love us so, have you allowed us to experience such pain?" As a social worker, I have observed some of the most incomprehensible situations where people have survived and I asked God time and time again, "WHY?" Yet, He continues to answer with the words... pain releases My anointing, suffering brings you to Me, and adversity breed's strength. It is a sad reality, but a truth worth storing away. I began to look over my life and commenced to observing the days I was closest to God. I discovered the correlation between the times in my life when I was going through tests (experiencing pain and suffering). These were the times when I was closest to God. Although, I was reluctant to admit it, God knew what was best for me. It remains too difficult to admit while in the test, but much like the three Hebrew boys, you must believe that once you enter the fiery furnace, God will have prepared a place for you in the presence of your enemy. So why have we believed the lie, that once we receive the message of Christ and all His blessings, everything was going to be perfect? Who told us this and why do we continue to expect it and believe in it? I have come to a place where I seem to understand a portion of this fallacy. We, in this existence anxiously wait for and expect some magical/spiritual event to occur before we allow ourselves to be released into the things of God and His purpose. We have believed and assumed that when we finally reach that place in God that there will be no more problems, sorrows, or heart aches; does this sound familiar? Many think that Christianity is some magical potion that is going to make everything all right, but this not so. As Christians, we must be reminded that our belief system in Christianity is a way of life. This is often obscured. I don't know about you, but the wait for the great emotional release from pain became laborious; as it did not happen for me! In search of the right timing, the right feeling of "ok", left me "disappointed" when the feeling did not live up to the high expectations of what I believed it would yield. This confused me. I encourage each reader to know that there is a feeling. This is especially true for the many readers who have had the charismatic Christian experience. However, the truth of the religion is that if you never feel anything and know in your heart that Jesus is the only begotten Son of the

Father who died and rose again from the grave on the third day, you are saved. Do the work to develop your soul and hold on to every promise in the written word of God. Go and do what is in your heart and bring Him glory. It is the receiving of His Lordship and permitting Him to rule in your mind, heart and will that separates you from the world. We are a people set apart for His divine use, not just for an emotional experience when we gather in the assembly, or when we set our individual times of prayer. I challenge you in this hour to know Him. It is only those who know Him that make it into His kingdom. It is not the works or the feelings, He seeks those who want to commune with Him. I urge you to not get caught in seeking the trapping of a modern day religious experience and miss the reason and the object of your worship. This temporal experience in the earth is not to be compared to the thing that He is working out in us for His use in the Kingdom He is preparing.

Nevertheless, I started this journey because I wanted so bad to receive that ok feeling. There is also another misconception that I have found in myself and many other believers, that once Jesus comes in He is going to make everything better. As a child, I always wanted to "fit in," but I never could find that, so I got saved and received Christ as my Lord and Savior. Not a bad deal; but that appeared to make things worse. In my attempt to get better or be more normal, I got worse. Now I was really different. But, I learned that even in the midst of our struggles, Christ is right there. Listen to the voice of the Lord calling us to get closer. He says to us, *draw nigh unto me and I will...* you fill it in. God has the desire to fulfill the longing in your soul. We have to allow ourselves to enter the place where He can speak to it. This means that we must open up to the truth often hidden within us. I have experienced that some unbelievers, and many believers, struggle as a result of 'faulty thinking'—-so focus on what has been postulated as a restrictive belief system. God says you can and can't do this or that. Not knowing that the truth is, Christ has come that we might have life, to set us free from the bondage of sin and death. It is only in Him that this rest exists. Many other beliefs can offer a pseudo rest in the earth realm, but true peace is found only in Christ Jesus who offers eternal peace both now and in the life to come. He declares, "I am the true vine, the only way to the Father. There is no other door or way to enter into this peace that I am speaking about.

I encourage you not to be blinded. I declare, all other ground is sinking sand.

During some of my lowest periods in this life, I can recall peaceful memories with God. I have yet to discover (and maybe never will) the reason why God has chosen the struggles of this world to perfect us, but know this; He promises to be a present help in the time of storm. It is the word that declares many are the afflictions of the righteous but the Lord delivers from them ALL. God is faithful to the journey that He has set for us to travel, and as a good leader, has traveled this road without sin and declares that we can accomplish this way in His strength.

Through all of this walking in the dark by faith and not sight, I have seen some Christians misinterpret the position with God. They think and believe that God has some how forsaken them or that they must be in sin or being punished for some past sin, but fail to see how close they are being brought to God in their trouble times. This is important. God chose us from the beginning, and you must know that you have not failed Him. We are caught off guard at our sins and shortcomings, but God is not surprised! Relax. We must let God do what He wants to accomplish in our lives, if for no other reason than He is going to have it His way. He's God and that is just the way it is!

Chapter 6

The Place of Worship

The Place of Worship

The place of worship
Not always the bowing of knees
Not just the lifting of hands
It is the surrendering of the heart, to God, to hear....
Maybe He wants to speak or...
Maybe there's a release for your heart
O, whatever a place you'll always find "peace"
You must know that to worship is to adore
To give reverence to pay homage to love forevermore
It's not just a moment, but it's an understanding
Our God is in control....
So, take your position
Relax walk out what your here for
Go bring Him honor
Bring Him glory
Love forevermore.... The place of Worship

James T. Freeman
Copyright © 2005 jtf95 Music

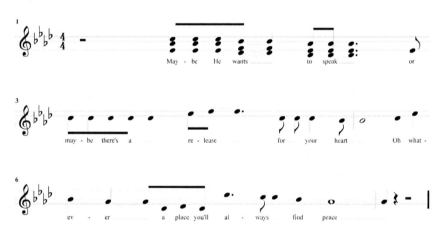

As we continue to see, year after year, people flock to conferences and seminars looking for the word of God to release them into the fullness of His word and their purpose in the earth, it is clear that Christians are struggling with accessing and maximizing the truth of God's word. We continue Sunday after Sunday, year after year, generation after generation believing and praying for the blessing of God to be revealed to us. The hope of the believer is demonstrated with each unrealized expectation or goal. What are we doing with this information? Do we continue in the hope? Do we just keep the faith? Could it be that God is trying to get us to do more? Face the truth; the word is nigh thee even in your mouth,[48] the earth is waiting for the true ones to manifest. Those are the sons of God who know in their hearts the Kingdom has been prepared for them and know that faith alone will produce nothing. The challenge for the Christian today is to discover, *what I need to do!* Our belief is a settled issue; but what are we willing to contribute in the process of bringing the word to pass? Personally, I have struggled in myself and with other believers of the faith who in their hope believed that God, the Pastor,

---

[48]Roman 10:8 & Deuteronomy 30:14

the Prophet, or visiting ministry would shoulder the responsibility of pushing through what they believe for from God. This also has been a place where I have had to allow God to speak truth into my spirit. Once we receive the word in the spirit, our faith must be put into action. Believers then must be instructed in the truth that will bring what they believe for into the earth realm. The truth will be the daily carrying out of what we declare we believe for from God. It is in this action, the day to day walking in the promise settled in the heart that our belief is made manifest, and after being made manifest, it can be tried then proven and given the opportunity for growth. I am sadden at the reality of how many do not see the goodness of God in the land of the living as a result of our inabilities, unwillingness, or lack of information on the importance of our role in word, deed, and faith. Remember, faith without works is dead.[49] The Christian cannot bring the purpose of God to pass in their life with faith alone. It is our opportunity as believers to hold on to faith when the next step is difficult to see, or our strength grows weak; but if we are not doing something we will not see the purpose of God fulfilled in us to its maximum potential.

---

[49]James 2:18; 20-26

It is in doing that something that God sees our faith in action to what we believe He has placed in our hearts. Consider again for a moment the parable of the talents. The servant with one talent hid his in the ground thinking, *I will return to the Master that which he gave.* As a result, the Master's response was, *you wicked and lazy servant, depart from me I knew you not.* We, as fellow believers in today's Christian community, must honestly consider if we are truly sharing, preparing and contributing to the fullest extent, or if we simply are waiting or looking for God to open doors, walk us through and hand deliver that which we are believing to be performed on our behalf. The unfortunate truth is that we absolve ourselves of the responsibility and look to acquisition without the accountability to pay the price. If this is not you, then praise God for your development on the path. What is frightening is the number of individuals who, continue through life with a dream, never push the envelope to see what their true ability could really release in the earth with God's help. How many of us are considering the cost, or how we are going to achieve, what God has placed in our spirits? It is this process that begins the qualifying factor to get to know Him. I find it interesting that the Master declares to the lazy servant who did nothing with the talent he was assigned that he "knew him not." This word is spoken as if in the process of getting to know the Master there is something that pushes you to do something with the talent He has given you that maximizes. Believers, do you see it? Your desire to know Him will push you to try. As your soul develops within you, there is something growing that is strengthened and awakens a quest to discover, *why did God call me into the earth, and what, am I to do?*

In the path of our destiny there is a price for the "dream." I tend to believe that we may consider the price, and this may even be the reason some never make the journey. There are few individuals who live out all of what God has declared and what we perceive as the opportunity to advance the purpose of the kingdom of God in the earth. I know that there are those who have set their hearts and minds to the task and are pushing forward. However, the vast majority of believers are caught between the desire for milk and the need to consume meat.[50] Hear again the scripture, as the voice of the scribes of God shared this truth, that

---

[50]Hebrew 5:12

man, in his fallen state, often trail behind and move at a much slower rate than what we could actually obtain in Christ.[51] There is something that is in the nature of man that is working in opposition to each meager attempt to move from the position of merely existing to maximizing the fullness of God's promises in the earth.

This chapter will examine worship as a life style or conscious decision the believer must make. It is the decision to stand on the position that God is in control and knows what He is doing! Can you risk the belief that God knows the thoughts He thinks in reference to you?[52] In this moment, speak to yourself and declare the purpose of God. Let your soul know, *"He will bring you to the expected end He has declared for you in His purpose.* Clearly, during the test or even on our routine everyday journey, we face the challenge of making the decision to trust in God's purpose and plan for our lives when confronting what appears to be unreasonable non-purposed pain. In these moments, understand it is a struggle to hear the word of faith. Still, there remains a group of Christian worshippers who are demanding in this hour, *God please, not another word declaring it is*

---

[51]Luke 16:8
[52]Jeremiah 29:11

working for my good; or a word confirming God is up to something." Christians today and those of yesterday want answers. Hear the cry of believers; *do we not serve a God who knows all things, is all loving...? Will He not answer us? Will he not fulfill our desire, the longing in our soul?* This is the heart's cry I hear in today's worshippers. I see a people who are ready for a move of God despite what has taken place in the church over the past several decades. These worshippers are crying out for glory. It is the heart of these members of the body, to be fully consumed with the purpose of God and the ability to see Him, His acts and His face, in this present day. These individuals, in search of God in this modern society, are in desperate need for more than another religious experience. I am excited; as the expectations and desires of the people develop, we will continue to see more of God in action. It is almost as if we as believers abandoned our understanding that God, in His infinite wisdom, limited His work in the earth to our belief and expectation. It is unto us as we believe. There is power at work in us that must be challenged, sharpened, and used to tap into exceeding abundantly above all. It is time out for Christians who never maximize the fullness of the experience God. Think about it; as mentioned earlier, there are generations of believers who have gone on and left this hope that, *maybe the next generation will do it.* Why is this? I would submit that God is willing but waits for us to come to our senses. Stop for a moment; take this opportunity to examine your thinking. What is it that you believe for? What is it that you are holding God hostage to and never seeing materialize?

Consider this: God is waiting for you to declare it, and you are waiting on Him. The word declares the earth is waiting for the "true sons[53]" to manifest and that the word is nigh thee even in your mouth. I want to see a place where we as Christians experience healing in this *new day.* This is the season that God is declaring "Walk free" of all those conditions, things, mental images, negative expectations or whatever the case may be. This is the time for Christians to begin to declare that there is a place of peace for all who will keep their minds stayed on Him. Fellow believers, can you believe God as He says to us,[54] "Your ability to keep your peace is a choice?" The place of worship is yours for inhabitation. We can choose to live life with the

[53]Romans 8:18-21
[54]Isaiah 26:3

awareness that He is in control and has given us many choices, and only requires that we in Him give Him the credit. This is worship. Think about it for a moment; how many of us still consider worship the point in the church service when the singers sing or the slow reverent song that causes everyone to cry or to lift their hands? It is my hope we can be challenged to move beyond this interpretation to the greater interpretation of worship as the choice to know that our God is in control. This powerful truth can lead us to the freedom to experience this life without inhibition, yet with limitation. We are the sacrifice He desires. I want to provide the opportunity for the reader to discover the power of being in Christ, yet being able to live to the point that it is Christ that lives through you. Dr. Youngblood teaches the worshippers at our local assembly, that the most acceptable offering to offer the Lord in worship is Himself. Can you see it? The thing we are after in this existence is to become like Him. Our quest, if you will, is to become the image we behold in the glass. Challenge yourself, take another moment, what are you beholding? Is it Jesus? Are you focusing on His purpose in the earth and how what He has put in you furthers His agenda to bring all men into the kingdom of God?

This is the place of worship. The surrendering of your will to hear and to do; in this place you will find the peace unexplainable. I have seen so many individuals in the name of the most liberating religion, Christianity, miss life. Do you really think God is pleased? These individuals, now turned sour, thinking they have missed out on something, unable to hear the freedom of God's word declare the entire garden is yours for exploration; do not sit focusing on the things we are instructed not to touch. Please be clear, I am not instructing or suggesting that there should be an abandonment of the truth of God's word or his plan for a sanctified existence. Consequently, there is a need to understand His plan for salvation and sanctification. Christian leaders in this new day have to reintroduce the communication about the process in which God employs to bring us to the place where we cry "Abba." Remember, He loves us to repentance. While we were sinners,[55] the God I speak of sent His only begotten son to die for us. It is necessary for Christian leaders and members of the body of Christ to declare this truth. God calls; all we can do is respond. His mercy and favor is something no one can merit, for all have sinned

---

[55]Romans 5:8

and do fall short.[56] We are currently in a time where so many positions of faith have arisen and individuals who seek truth and peace are vulnerable to false doctrine and false truth. Stand up. We are set apart by Him for His purpose. Know the truth, declare the truth, it will make you free. All we have to do is lift Him up, He will draw all men. If we create the sound, those who hear it will respond.

We reside in a generation that is in hot pursuit of quick fixes, immediate responses and successes without paying the price. Pay attention to the current marketing; get your degree in 18 months, go to school on your own time without going to class via the internet, or the now classic, "you can get immediate approval call today!" all pointing to the buy-now-pay-later concept.

I believe that we are approaching a move of God that will thrust us forward yet challenge us to comprehend the benefit of the two fruits, *patience* and *long suffering*. Those who will continue on this journey must come to a place where the decision is firm, *I just can't give up.* There is a determination that is available to believers in

[56]Romans 3:23

this hour. It is time for the mature in Christ to rise up. No more just sitting back waiting in the name of God...we must take our position. Consider this; God is waiting on you. It is sad to know that many have died waiting on God, but could not hear the voice of God say, *in My strength go and do."* We must walk it out. The purpose of God is for us to bring him glory...I challenge us to examine what's in our treasure[57]...what has He hidden in you that will bring Him glory and honor? There is a truth we often forget and God has been trying to get us to see it from the beginning. There is an entire garden prepared, if you don't watch and pray you will get caught up focused on the one tree you've been instructed not to eat of while there are so many other options to explore. This is a powerful truth I revisit often. There is a garden full of options... God waits for us to explore. All He wants is the credit. How many of us still today refuse to experience life in the name of God? Those who declare, "I'm waiting on God to say"... stop. Can you now hear God say, *I'm waiting on you?*

---

[57] 2 Corinthians 4:7

I am convinced that once we surrender our hearts to God, anything we do will bring Him glory. Let's take a pause to pull it all together. The question we are examining is, *what does growing the soul really mean?* I would suggest that there is a position in the earth that God desires for every believer. It is in this position that He expects for the believer to have great fulfillment and success. As a worshiper, I personally believe that the secret to growing the soul is learning to worship. Once the process of worship is birthed in a person, the process of complete self denial for the purpose of a greater source take place. for the Christian this source is God. From this place anything can happen. The believer taps into a source and strength that is beyond their comprehension. Supernatural power becomes available. This is why I believe John would declare from the very thought of the Father: *above all things, I wish that you would prosper even as your soul prospers.* Therefore, there are several steps we consider in growing the soul and dwelling in the place of worship.

In **step one, *reconnection,*** there is a response to the call of God in faith that energizing an act of will. This is what we have (to this point) experienced as the emerging of the soul with its immature selfish emotional responses. In this step we encounter the opportunity to make a choice to believe; this choice then releases the new paradigm that, *everything I go through and experience is working for His good, and has purpose.* In **step two, rest,** we behold the opportunity to enter into the rest God has prepared for the believer in the earth. After we believe and act, God reveals His power. The door then opens to the rest prepared. Once we receive the revelation, we must make an additional response to His position of being in control. This response is the positioning of ourselves as worshippers. This is the place where we come to the understanding that God is in control. Finally, in **step three, *responsibility,*** we are challenge to walk out the purpose of our existence and to bring God glory with our labor. This is the place where you here Him say, "Relax, walk out what you're here for." As we approach the conclusion, I encourage you not to lose heart; your ability to bring Him glory and honor is your purpose. Please, discontinue the labor intensive work we do to discover the mystery of our existence. I declare with the scriptures, we were made to give God glory and honor! Believers, let's demonstrate to the world who we are in our Father's strength. I want to end the needless deaths and miscarriages of purpose due to this mystical search that prevents the real work necessary to move the agenda of God for the believers. I remind you that we have ceased from our own labor, found a place of rest, and now it is our duty and joy to offer worship. The act of giving God back that which He has given us.

EVEN AS THE SOUL

Conclusion

A HOLY LIFE

Holy Life

Jesus went to Calvary
To save a wretch like you- like me
Still men don't know why He died...
In this life
He promised me
A life to live
Abundantly
A holy life
For me to live
Both day and night
All through the year
To be Holy as I am Holy says the Lord
Just long to be Holy as I am Holy says the Lord

In a world of much confusion
Where people are dying and in despair
How do we find the solution?
To show them that you care
I hurt to know their hurting
I'm afraid to know their fear
A people lost and in confusion
Bond and can't seem to be set free
Lord I am not simply asking why me
But I long to be...
Holy as I am Holy says the Lord

In this life
He promised me
That He would help me to believe
That He would keep this heart of mine
And He would help me through the hardest time
To be...Holy as I am Holy says the Lord

James T. Freeman
Copyright © 2005 jtf95 Music

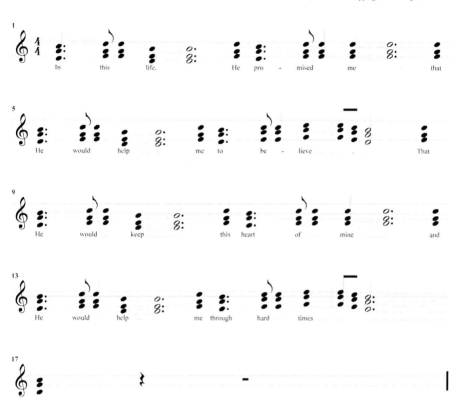

I n my effort to conclude this portion of the journey, I have discovered many different truths that continue to challenge me to examine the basic truth of God's word. I conclude that outside of Him there is nothing... that is, NO-thing can exist. In many instances, individuals become caught up in the mere existence and operation of this world; experience the casualty of seeing the development of a deeper meaning and understanding of this life as unimportant. In essence, they continue to look for ways to be independent and to prosper, not understanding that independent of others, our growth is limited. Consequently, their focus remains selfish and limited to the here and now. They seek temporal success and desire ways in which to make money. This individualistic and capitalistic mind set is in direct opposition to the will of the Father. In the scriptures, God is constantly pointing the believer to the role of fellowship and right relationship with fellow believers in the earth. The scriptures advocate this position so strongly, that the love of self is tied to your ability to love your brother. Even so, the New Testament cautions us with the question of, "how can we love God who we have not seen and be challenged in our love for our brother who we see in the flesh?"[58] I encourage

[58] 1 John 4:20

each reader to examine how much God has gone through to love you as an individual. He gave His life, He remembers your sin no more after you repent and He has love and mercy that is renewed each day. These are the acts of a loving Father who in building the foundation for His family in the earth, continues to strengthen the system through love. This is the revelation revealed to the New Testament church that the whole law can be summed up in the ability to love others as you love yourself. The believer must know that the love we are receiving, He desires for us to love others in the same manner. How powerful. The love we receive has been given to us that we might, in His strength, show Him to someone else with that same love. often say that God, in His wisdom, declares this truth; if we receive the understanding of how to love as He loved us, then and only then, can the whole of the law be summed up in the principle "love your neighbor as you love yourself." I declare that we are not equipped to love ourselves until we know the love of God. It is after experiencing this kind of love that empowers us to love in His strength and to shift our focus from self preservation to kingdom expansion. In the strength of His love, the believer moves from the strength of the world system of love and motivation for self preservation. Until this occurs, the believer must be cautioned that the love of God is to be birthed first in them before it can be given out. The equipping of the believer to share the love of God is a process. This journey has been an attempt to introduce the readers to a portion of this process. The journey inward is most often one of the most difficult. As indicated earlier, the heart is desperately wicked and its true intent is often not revealed. The best we can do is to attempt to discover the love of God and mimic this love in our relationship to our brothers in the earth.

It has been my experience that some individuals seek prosperity or what appears to be wealth in their search for security and material gain. These are all important in the process of maturing; nevertheless, they cannot be the focus of the Christian's walk of faith. The challenge for the believer then becomes this: *once I receive the promise of God in the earth, how do I put it to work for the kingdom?* We must not forget to bring Him glory. Once we begin to seek our own glory or attempt to establish something for ourselves, we assume ownership and in our action deny that He is God enough to keep His promise that He would supply all our needs according to His riches.[59] I am in no way attempting to prevent anyone from planning for him or herself, their families or their future. I believe that is a very important concept, and God is pleased when we are organized enough to establish such things in the earth. The principle I am attempting to share relates more to the understanding of one's purpose in God. This book has endeavored to present to the reader that God wants you, all of you, and that we need Him. The good, the bad, the happy and the sad, He is working it all for good to an end He declared in the beginning. Thus, once you receive this truth, and experience the life changing power that accompanies, He is heart broken when you do not ensure that others hear, know and experience this love He is trying to get in the earth to others through you.

Often as a child, I would hear the Lord whisper in my ear that there is more to this life than living and dying. I thought to myself, "What does this mean?" In this life there are so many opportunities to do and become more... It is so easy to forget that we have been made

---

[59]Philippians 4:19

in the image of a God who declares "all things are possible." We must believe the unbelievable, dream the unthinkable and reach the unreachable[60] because it is our creative right in that we were created in His image. How often do we ask ourselves, "what would I do if..." Why would we in the face of challenges, determine to face them head on with a determination to win/conquer whatever the obstacle? The consistent walking in the truth of God's word has taught me to understand "easy street" does not exist. The search for this easy street causes many people that would and could make a difference, to relax and become comfortable with the status quo. Personally, I don't think there is anything wrong with satisfaction, but for those who are pulled to do more or hear the call for greatness, they can be hindered by the force and power of ease/satisfaction. The spirit of apathy or the relaxation of status quo holds the believer back from moving forward. How do we determine if we fit into the category? Each reader must know their position, so ask, *"Am I the one who is satisfied or at ease? Am I the one who has reached a place where the push no longer makes sense? Or am I refraining from the extra effort experiencing the*

---

[60]Commissioned 1999

[61]The desire to move forward that is hindered by emotional issues of the past. James Freeman

blockage of will[61]?" There is no easy answer. This answer is unique for each believer. We often look for others to provide for us only what we can, in our relationship with God the Father, provide for ourselves. I encourage every reader to examine your life challenges, and what you have experienced; see what the common threads are that pull together and help you give this life meaning. What are the things that occurred in your life that make you cry? Could it be God making you sensitive to Him and the needs of His people? Reflect on this; God loves you so much that He would challenge you to walk through the valley. Then while you are in the valley He declares, *I am going to go through with you, keep you while you're going through after it is over charging you to use the experience as a testimony.* This life of separation to God is not in our strength; again, it is in Him and only in Him we can survive.

Wealth has for so long been the desired end of the temporal experience we know in the flesh. It is the hope, dream and motivation for many. Unfortunately, the prosperity movement has left numerous Christians pondering whether or not they have truly received a word from God during this move as a result of their inability to materialize the promised riches. I encourage you…. Don't loose the faith God has spoken. Recall; we move from faith to faith, glory to glory, here a little there a little,[62] with it all working together for our good as we continue to love and serve the Lord. However, now the challenge has arrived and our faith must stand the test. The scriptures ring true in that many Christians perish for the lack of knowledge. Too many Christians are looking for prosperity as a check in the mail, the winning of the sweepstakes, or some other means for which no effort of their own was sacrificed. As a result, the true move of God is most often missed. It has recently come to my attention, as I have grown in Christ, that prosperity is closely related to the growth of the person. One truly experiences prosperity when he can recognize "I am not the same, I have changed." It is this truth that we take for granted and misinterpret the plan of God for our growth. Still believing God for the check in the mail is ineffective if you are never nurturing the new man or woman that is emerging created by God for the purpose of the blessing. Remember, He created the blessing to bless you. Consequently, losing

---

[62]Isaiah 28:13

focus on the true plan of God to prosper even as the soul prospers causes the believer to get off course. God is attempting to make you a new person who is strong enough mentally, physically and spiritually to acquire with His help the necessary skills and tools needed to posses the land. Can you recall God's original plan? He purposed man to have dominion, rule, conquer and to subdue. We are the children of God who were created as priestly members of the royal family- the peculiar nation. This truth is so easy to forget that in the midst of our rapidly moving society that the God that we serve remains the same. We, in our humanness and members of this rapidly moving 21st century, expect the promises of God to take on the same level of speed that everything else in this microwave society has, but He in His wisdom continues to build patience in us. This, as He has originally instructed, was one of the fruits of His spirit. Along with patience, He is building in us the capacity to operate at the next level as we mature in both soul and spirit. Think about it, if it is prosperity that He promised then there is so much more that we as individuals must learn. Imagine for a moment the blessing being given to us in our ill prepared state. I am often reminded of the plan of God in the scripture that declares to him that is faithful over little I (our God) will make him the ruler of plenty.

God is creating a new system, one that is different from the world's system, equipping the individual for the forth-coming prosperity, what ever it may be … money, wisdom, knowledge or some other form of ministry. If it is the belief that this prosperity is coming from God, the question becomes, *why has he chosen this for you?* We must understand that God never just blesses us for ourselves, but for ministry. We recall again, He is the God that declares that all things work together for the good of them who He loved and called. This again speaks to the unity of the believers. Everything is working together for our good. It is so easy for us to forget that God has declared the end from the beginning. He in, His infinite mercy, employed His foreknowledge before He predestined, thus He knew everything that would happen and then He designed our existence. What a mighty God!

As mature Christians, we have to "grow up" and learn to meet the needs of the body. Emerging into the fullness of the concept that, *God is the provider*, the source; but we are the instruments He uses to bring His word to pass. We must also embrace the knowledge that it is through the obedience of the tithes and offerings that God begins to open up vision and plants the seed of faith in us. He is instilling in us the principles of the family vision. It is once we settle this belief, that the activities of this truth in our hearts prepare us for receiving greater revelation, that we are positioned to receive vision. At this point, vision is conceived and after conceived, we will have the strength to give birth only by standing firm in the position we will have seen and experienced of the Father. We can only become what we have beheld. It is then that God speaks and ones faith is challenged to move forward trusting and believing in a Father, who we have seen bring His word to past. Do not miss the opportunity to receive the manifest blessings of God in the earth. Dare to believe beyond your own strength and ability. Stop limiting God to the events that take place on Sunday, and boxing Him into communication that can only take place in the church or with a spiritual representative such as the preacher or priest. Can you just hear God saying, *You could have so much more?* Nevertheless, it is rather frightening to me that most of creation will miss it when God wants so desperately to give Himself to us. Consequently, they will miss not only the opportunity to know the more of God—-the relationship, the peace, the protection, the provision but that they will miss it due to the unwillingness to settle this information within the heart. The bible speaks to the problem this way: "men fall as a result of lack of knowledge.[63]" What is frightening is that people are not in search of truth. I urge each reader to remember this truth, God satisfies the hungry soul and satisfies those who are in search; for all who seek shall find. God takes pleasure in revealing Himself to those who are hungry. Therefore, it is critical, that we as a Christian family do better with bearing the infirmity of the weak and shouldering the burdens of them who can not carry their own weight. There are many who never get from under the stress of their everyday existence and remain focused on the pains and woes of this life. They are not able alone to find the strength to declare, *all things are working together for my good.* It is often forgotten and not stressed that this walk, though it be an individual journey, is not a walk that is rewarded if you make it alone. The scriptures do not make reference to a prize being placed on the lone ranger, but rather the taking of that individual's solitude and placing him into

[63]Hosea 4:6

families. Hear the song, "we are created together, you and me, we are the body of Jesus Christ His son. We are joined in this family to walk in unity…" God does have a purpose. So often in life we are journeying and it seems so futile, as if we are traveling just for the sake of traveling. This perspective has caused many to lose heart; to faint in their well doing, yielding a missed harvest as their season had passed on, and they were not in the space or the place to receive the blessing. It is hard for us to believe that God would not bless us or that there are contingencies on the retrieval of blessing. I submit again, that one of the most important lessons we are learning in the earth is to rule and have dominion. We as believers are being transformed to the image of the son in the earth.[64] Are you ready? And, as the ultimate power, He does not release this ability to one who does not learn the basics of submission, obedience, patience and longsuffering. Think in the natural; a father does not release to his son responsibility and resources before he believes him to have achieved readiness. The supervisor does not recommend promotion until the employee has demonstrated growth in the position and the ability to

---

[64] 2 Corinthians 3:18

assume more and the banks most often will not release a loan outside of the demonstrated reliability of an individual's credit worthiness demonstrated by their past credit.

I close with this thought; my soul is grounded in the only thing I know to be true and that is Christ Jesus. I believe that through my life experiences, I have gained tremendous respect for the word of God. This reminds us of "seasons" and how seasons come and go, growing and nurturing new seed, as well as increasing the strength of the roots that are rooted and grounded in the faith of the Lord Jesus (His promise remains that we shall be like trees planted by the rivers of water that shall not be moved bearing fruit in DUE SEASON!).[65] It is hard when you are in trouble or going through a trial to comprehend that God has a time for the things that are in your spirit. There is also a difficulty that we face when we must hear God say to us; *your trials come to make you strong.* I continue to hear Him declare to us through the word (Romans 5:3) "…Knowing tribulation works patience and patience, experience; and experience, hope…" There is an understanding of the

---

[65]Psalm 1

process that the Christian must have that supercedes the experiences of this life. Our hope MUST be built on the knowledge of Jesus and His righteousness. There is something ever so sweet in the phrase, "He is all my righteousness, I stand complete in Him!" The enemy continues to attempt to rob us of our inheritance in Him. In this moment, allow God to speak to you and command the revival of your spirit and life to your soul. These members of your person are waiting to come alive! You can tell your story better than anyone else could ever speak it into the atmosphere. How often have you sat around feeling the desire for that thing you could not put words to, the feeling that there was something MORE, that something was pulling on you demanding that you keep on, in spite of and regardless to whatever. If you have read to this point, you know what I am talking about. The feeling of this expectation for *more*, the belief for the unbelievable, the hope for the exceeding abundantly above is sometimes overwhelming; and when we don't see the expected result we, are forced to fight with the desire to give up. I urge you, don't settle for complacency or despair, don't give up hope. Settle the truth of His word, "for He satisfies the longing soul, and fills the hungry soul with goodness" (Psalms 107:9) He is going to bring His word to pass. I declare there is a remnant of believers that God is about to call an assembly for that will shake the foundation of the earth and demonstrate to all men, and to generations to come, that He will do just what He said. I too have struggled to keep the faith not to lose heart; thoughts of throwing in the towel. Each time, I could still hear the tender voice of the Lord calling. He would simply declare, *you will reap if you faint not.* If there is no other message you receive, then hear this; there is a shift in this season. God is opening the portals of the heavens for those who have kept their ears inclined to hear from Him, not just to what a vessel in the kingdom had declared as His oracle. Those who have desired to know His voice and desired to follow after His will. Hear again God say to us, *Relax, I am in control!*

I do believe that I have come to understand that what ever I do will prosper and it is not so much about what I should and need to do, as this is often transient and will change, more so than it is the simple act of doing something in His name. The word instructs us, "Whatever it is we do, do it with our whole heart as unto the Lord…" I've spent so much time and energy in attempting to develop; either in education, religion, or employment, all in preparation to experience what I felt God was going to give me *some day*. However, I could never hear God say to me what I hear in this hour, *live the dream!* To my surprise, this word presents itself when I am at a point of confusion, desperation and in need of encouragement. At least that is what I thought. As the words of the old adage declare, *He may not come when you want Him, but He is always on time.* I have been walking with the Lord since I was eight years of age, I have seen good days, bad days; I have had mountain top experiences as well as valley lows all to get me to the place where I declare with the word, "Godliness with contentment is great gain." I have decided that the Lord is my strength and I can only live the life He is requiring of me in and through Him.

There are several scriptural references listed in this book and principles that I have discovered to aide me in my walk with Christ. I encourage each reader to examine the scriptures; there is life that is waiting for you. God is again looking to get into the earth through your work. There is a mandate for the believers who receive the truth that we are the sons of God, in the earth to expand His kingdom. This task is accomplished in our ability to model what we have seen and received of the Father in the development of our inner man the soul. As believers, we are taught in our local assembly, Higher Call World Outreach, that the equipping of believers for kingdom expansion is birthed from father to son. Consider for example the training of Adam, the first son in the earth. He, after being instructed by the Father on the rules of expanding the kingdom, named and declared a purpose over all functioning members in the earth. This pleased the Father. God is in need of you; He needs your hands, your feet, your ideas… will you help the world to see the greatness of our God? I challenge you to prosper as your soul prospers. I charge each of the situations and experiences you go through to release to you, wisdom from the heart of God. Declare to your soul, *I will grow. I am no longer going to allow situations, experiences, or people to enter in and out of my life without searching out what was the assignment.* God is waiting to reveal His purpose to us. Embrace the special position we hold in Him. This is the true Holy Life I declare for the Christian to embrace in this hour. We have been set apart for His divine use.

He has been longing to demonstrate to the world that, *those who are called by My name represent a glorious church.* Are you ready for this move? In this hour, everything we do will bring Him glory. I encourage you to submit to God and receive the assurance that all you do will prosper. There may still be someone who is asking, "What do I have to give God that will bring glory?" I suggest you look in your heart, then in your hand. God has given each of us a measure for which to bring Him glory. Just do something! My friend, please do not despise a small beginning. If we do not start, we will never give Him the opportunity to enlarge the place of our dwelling.

Scriptures

Introduction: Can I See You Again?

Proverb 4:7 Wisdom [is] the principal thing; [therefore] get
wisdom: and with all thy getting get understanding.
The living translation: 7 Getting wisdom is the most important thing
you can do! And whatever else you do, get good judgment.

3 John 1:2 Beloved, I wish above all things that thou mayest
prosper and be in health, even as thy soul prospereth.

James 2:23 And the scripture was fulfilled which saith, Abraham
believed God, and it was imputed unto him for
righteousness: and he was called the Friend of God.
The living translation-
James 2:23 And so it happened just as the Scriptures say:
"Abraham believed God, so God declared him to be
righteous." He was even called "the friend of God." So you
see, we are made right with God by what we do, not by
faith alone.

Chapter One: Your Mercy

Philippians 2: 13 for it is God which worketh in you both to will
and to do of [his] good pleasure.
(TLT)2:13 For God is working in you, giving you the desire to obey
him and the power to do what pleases him.
Romans 8:28 And we know that all things work together for good
to them that love God, to them who are the called
according to [his] purpose.

Luke 12:32 Fear not, little flock; for it is your Father's good
pleasure to give you the kingdom.

(TLT)12:32 "So don't be afraid, little flock. For it gives your Father
great happiness to give you the Kingdom."

Ephesians 1:5 & 9   Having predestinated us unto the adoption of children by Jesus Christ to himself, according to the good pleasure of his will,

Ephesians 1:6   To the praise of the glory of his grace, wherein he hath made us accepted in the beloved.

Ephesians 1:7   In whom we have redemption through his blood, the forgiveness of sins, according to the riches of his grace;

Ephesians 1:8   Wherein he hath abounded toward us in all wisdom and prudence;

Ephesians 1:9   Having made known unto us the mystery of his will, according to his good pleasure which he hath purposed in himself:

The living translation- 5 His unchanging plan has always been to adopt us into his own family by bringing us to himself through Jesus Christ. And this gave him great pleasure.
6 So we praise God for the wonderful kindness he has poured out on us because we belong to his dearly loved Son. 7 He is so rich in kindness that he purchased our freedom through the blood of his Son, and our sins are forgiven. 8 He has showered his kindness on us, along with all wisdom and understanding.
9 God's secret plan has now been revealed to us; it is a plan centered on Christ, designed long ago according to his good pleasure.

2 Thessalonians 1:11-12 Wherefore also we pray always for you, that our God would count you worthy of [this] calling, and fulfil all the good pleasure of [his] goodness, and the work of faith with power:
That the name of our Lord Jesus Christ may be glorified in you, and ye in him, according to the grace of our God and the Lord Jesus Christ.

Living Translation-11 And so we keep on praying for you, that our God will make you worthy of the life to which he called you. And we pray that God, by his power, will fulfill all your good intentions and faithful deeds. 12 Then everyone will give honor to the name of our Lord Jesus because of you, and you will be honored along with him. This is all made possible because of the undeserved favor of our God and Lord, Jesus Christ.

John 15:7 If ye abide in me, and my words abide in you, ye shall ask what ye will, and it shall be done unto you

Chapter Two: His Heart's Cry

Galatians 5: 13-14 For, brethren, ye have been called unto liberty; only [use] not liberty for an occasion to the flesh, but by love serve one another. For all the law is fulfilled in one word, [even] in this; Thou shalt love thy neighbor as thyself.
TLT-13 For you have been called to live in freedom-not freedom to satisfy your sinful nature, but freedom to serve one another in love. 14 For the whole law can be summed up in this one command: "Love your neighbor as yourself"

Luke 10:27 And he answering said, Thou shalt love the Lord thy God with all thy heart, and with all thy soul, and with all thy strength, and with all thy mind; and thy neighbour as thyself.

Luke 10:27 The man answered, " `You must love the Lord your God with all your heart, all your soul, all your strength, and all your mind.' And, `Love your neighbor as yourself.

Luke 1:37 For with God nothing shall be impossible.
Exodus
1 Corinthians 10:13- There hath no temptation taken you but such as is common to man: but God [is] faithful, who will not suffer you to be tempted above that ye are able; but will with the temptation also make a way to escape, that ye may be able to bear [it].
NLT-13 But remember that the temptations that come into your life are no different from what others experience. And God is faithful. He will keep the temptation from becoming so strong that you can't stand up against it. When you are tempted, he will show you a way out so that you will not give in to it.

Jeremiah 29:11- For I know the thoughts that I think toward you, saith the LORD, thoughts of peace, and not of evil, to give you an expected end.

NLT- For I know the thoughts that I think toward you, saith the LORD, thoughts of peace, and not of evil, to give you an expected end.

Numbers 13:30- And Caleb stilled the people before Moses, and said, Let us go up at once, and possess it; for we are well able to overcome it.

Philippians 4:13- I can do all things through Christ which strengtheneth me.

Chapter Three: Don't Want-to Die

2 Corinthians 12:9- And he said unto me, My grace is sufficient for thee: for my strength is made perfect in weakness. Most gladly therefore will I rather glory in my infirmities, that the power of Christ may rest upon me.

2 Corinthians 12:8-10; 8 Three different times I begged the Lord to take it away. 9 Each time he said, "My gracious favor is all you need. My power works best in your weakness." So now I am glad to boast about my weaknesses, so that the power of Christ may work through me. 10 Since I know it is all for Christ's good, I am quite content with my weaknesses and with insults, hardships, persecutions, and calamities. For when I am weak, then I am strong.

Hebrews 4: 9-12 There remaineth therefore a rest to the people of God. For he that is entered into his rest, he also hath ceased from his own works, as God [did] from his. Let us labor therefore to enter into that rest, lest any man fall after the same example of unbelief. For the word of God [is] quick, and powerful, and sharper than any two-edged sword, piercing even to the dividing asunder of soul and spirit, and of the joints and marrow, and [is] a discerner of the thoughts and intents of the heart.

NKT- 9 So there is a special rest* still waiting for the people of God. 10 For all who enter into God's rest will find rest from their labors, just as God rested after creating the world. 11 Let us do our

best to enter that place of rest. For anyone who disobeys God, as the people of Israel did, will fall.
12 For the word of God is full of living power. It is sharper than the sharpest knife, cutting deep into our innermost thoughts and desires. It exposes us for what we really are. 13 Nothing in all creation can hide from him. Everything is naked and exposed before his eyes. This is the God to whom we must explain all that we have done.

2 Corinthians 4:17- For our light affliction, which is but for a moment, worketh for us a far more exceeding [and] eternal weight of glory;

Romans 8:28 And we know that God causes everything to work together* for the good of those who love God and are called according to his purpose for them.

2 Corinthians 4:8-10 [We are] troubled on every side, yet not distressed; [we are] perplexed, but not in despair; Persecuted, but not forsaken; cast down, but not destroyed; Always bearing about in the body the dying of the Lord Jesus, that the life also of Jesus might be made manifest in our body.

Psalm 138:8- The LORD will perfect [that which] concerneth me: thy mercy, O LORD, [endureth] for ever: forsake not the works of thine own hands.

Job 1:8- And the LORD said unto Satan, Hast thou considered my servant Job, that [there is] none like him in the earth, a perfect and an upright man, one that feareth God, and escheweth evil?

Proverb 27:17- Iron sharpeneth iron; so a man sharpeneth the countenance of his friend.

Galatians 6:2 TLT- Dear brothers and sisters, if another Christian* is overcome by some sin, you who are godly should gently and humbly help that person back onto the right path. And be careful not to fall into the same temptation yourself. 2 Share each other's troubles and problems, and in this way obey the law of Christ. Brethren, if a man be overtaken in a fault, ye which are spiritual, restore such an one in the spirit of meekness; considering thyself, lest thou also be tempted. Bear ye one another's burdens, and so fulfill the law of Christ.

Hebrews 11

Romans 8:29 for whom he did foreknow, he also did predestinate [to be] conformed to the image of his Son, that he might be the firstborn among many brethren.

Romans 8:29 For God knew his people in advance, and he chose them to become like his Son, so that his Son would be the firstborn, with many brothers and sisters.

Chapter Four: Can't Give Up

Matthews 11:27 All things are delivered unto me of my Father: and no man knoweth the Son, but the Father; neither knoweth any man the Father, save the Son, and [he] to whomsoever the Son will reveal [him].

Matthews 11:28 Come unto me, all [ye] that labour and are heavy laden, and I will give you rest.

Matthews 11:29 Take my yoke upon you, and learn of me; for I am meek and lowly in heart: and ye shall find rest unto your souls.

Matthews 11:30 For my yoke [is] easy, and my burden is light.

27 "My Father has given me authority over everything. No one really knows the Son except the Father, and no one really knows the Father except the Son and those to whom the Son chooses to reveal him."

28 Then Jesus said, "Come to me, all of you who are weary and carry heavy burdens, and I will give you rest. 29 Take my yoke upon you. Let me teach you, because I am humble and gentle, and you will find rest for your souls. 30 For my yoke fits perfectly, and the burden I give you is light."

Philippians 1:6 Being confident of this very thing, that he which hath begun a good work in you will perform [it] until the day of Jesus Christ:

Philippians 1:6 And I am sure that God, who began the good work within you, will continue his work until it is finally finished on that day when Christ Jesus comes back again.

Isaiah 51:1 Hearken to me, ye that follow after righteousness, ye that seek the LORD: look unto the rock [whence] ye are hewn, and to the hole of the pit [whence] ye are digged.

A Call to Trust the Lord
"Listen to me, all who hope for deliverance-all who seek the Lord! Consider the quarry from which you were mined, the rock from which you were cut! 2 Yes, think about your ancestors Abraham and Sarah, from whom you came. Abraham was alone when I called him. But when I blessed him, he became a great nation."

Romans 8:37 Nay, in all these things we are more than conquerors through him that loved us.

Luke 12:32 Fear not, little flock; for it is your Father's good pleasure to give you the kingdom.

Isaiah 64:4 For since the beginning of the world [men] have not heard, nor perceived by the ear, neither hath the eye seen, O God, beside thee, [what] he hath prepared for him that waiteth for him.

1Crorinthians 2:9 But as it is written, Eye hath not seen, nor ear heard, neither have entered into the heart of man, the things which God hath prepared for them that love him.

Ephesians 3:20 Now unto him that is able to do exceeding abundantly above all that we ask or think, according to the power that worketh in us,

Ephesians 3:

20 Now glory be to God! By his mighty power at work within us, he is able to accomplish infinitely more than we would ever dare to ask or hope. 21 May he be given glory in the church and in Christ Jesus forever and ever through endless ages. Amen.

Chapter Five: The Place of Rest

Lamentation 3:
21 Yet I still dare to hope when I remember this:
22 The unfailing love of the Lord never ends! By his mercies we have been kept from complete destruction. 23 Great is his faithfulness; his mercies begin afresh each day. 24 I say to myself, "The Lord is my inheritance; therefore, I will hope in him!"
25 The Lord is wonderfully good to those who wait for him and seek him. 26 So it is good to wait quietly for salvation from the Lord. 27 And it is good for the young to submit to the yoke of his discipline.
28 Let them sit alone in silence beneath the Lord's demands. 29 Let them lie face down in the dust; then at last there is hope for them. 30 Let them turn the other cheek to those who strike them. Let them accept the insults of their enemies.
31 For the Lord does not abandon anyone forever. 32 Though he brings grief, he also shows compassion according to the greatness of his unfailing love. 33 For he does not enjoy hurting people or causing them sorrow.

Lam 3:21 This I recall to my mind, therefore have I hope.
Lam 3:22 [It is of] the LORD'S mercies that we are not consumed, because his compassions fail not.
Lam 3:23 [They are] new every morning: great [is] thy faithfulness.
Lam 3:24 The LORD [is] my portion, saith my soul; therefore will I hope in him.
Lam 3:25 The LORD [is] good unto them that wait for him, to the soul [that] seeketh him.
Lam 3:26 [It is] good that [a man] should both hope and quietly wait for the salvation of the LORD.

Zechariah 4:6 Then he answered and spake unto me, saying, This [is] the word of the LORD unto Zerubbabel, saying, Not by might, nor by power, but by my spirit, saith the LORD of hosts.

Philippians 4:6 Be careful for nothing; but in every thing by prayer and supplication with thanksgiving let your requests be made known unto God.

4 Always be full of joy in the Lord. I say it again-rejoice! 5 Let everyone see that you are considerate in all you do. Remember, the Lord is coming soon.
6 Don't worry about anything; instead, pray about everything. Tell God what you need, and thank him for all he has done. 7 If you do this, you will experience God's peace, which is far more wonderful than the human mind can understand. His peace will guard your hearts and minds as you live in Christ Jesus.
8 And now, dear brothers and sisters let me say one more thing as I close this letter. Fix your thoughts on what is true and honorable and right. Think about things that are pure and lovely and admirable. Think about things that are excellent and worthy of praise. 9 Keep putting into practice all you learned from me and heard from me and saw me doing, and the God of peace will be with you.

Hebrews 5
While Jesus was here on earth, he offered prayers and pleadings, with a loud cry and tears, to the one who could deliver him out of death. And God heard his prayers because of his reverence for God. 8 So even though Jesus was God's Son, he learned obedience from the things he suffered. 9 In this way, God qualified him as a perfect High Priest, and he became the source of eternal salvation for all those who obey him.

Chapter Six: The Place of Worship

Romans 10:8 But what saith it? The word is nigh thee, [even] in thy mouth, and in thy heart: that is, the word of faith, which we preach;

Deuteronomy 30:14 But the word [is] very nigh unto thee, in thy mouth, and in thy heart, that thou mayest do it.

James 2:20 But wilt thou know, O vain man, that faith without works is dead?

James 2:26 For as the body without the spirit is dead, so faith without works is dead also.

James 2:18 Yea, a man may say, Thou hast faith, and I have works: shew me thy faith without thy works, and I will shew thee my faith by my works.

Hebrews 5:12 For when for the time ye ought to be teachers, ye have need that one teach you again which [be] the first principles of the oracles of God; and are become such as have need of milk, and not of strong meat.

A Call to Spiritual Growth
11 There is so much more we would like to say about this. But you don't seem to listen, so it's hard to make you understand. 12 You have been Christians a long time now, and you ought to be teaching others. Instead, you need someone to teach you again the basic things a beginner must learn about the Scriptures.* You are like babies who drink only milk and cannot eat solid food. 13 And a person who is living on milk isn't very far along in the Christian life and doesn't know much about doing what is right. 14 Solid food is for those who are mature, who have trained themselves to recognize the difference between right and wrong and then do what is right.
Jeremiah 29:11 For I know the thoughts that I think toward you, saith the LORD, thoughts of peace, and not of evil, to give you an expected end.
Romans 8:19 For the earnest expectation of the creature waiteth for the manifestation of the sons of God.

18 Yet what we suffer now is nothing compared to the glory he will give us later. 19 For all creation is waiting eagerly for that future day when God will reveal who his children really are. 20 Against its will, everything on earth was subjected to God's curse. 21 All

creation anticipates the day when it will join God's children in glorious freedom from death and decay.

Isaiah 26:3 Thou wilt keep [him] in perfect peace, [whose] mind [is] stayed [on thee]: because he trusteth in thee.
Romans 5:8 But God commendeth his love toward us, in that, while we were yet sinners, Christ died for us.
Romans 3:23 For all have sinned, and come short of the glory of God;
2Corinthians 4:7 But we have this treasure in earthen vessels, that the excellency of the power may be of God, and not of us.

Chapter Seven: The Conclusion
"Holy Life"

1John 4:20 If a man say, I love God, and hateth his brother, he is a liar: for he that loveth not his brother whom he hath seen, how can he love God whom he hath not seen?

Philippians 4:19 But my God shall supply all your need according to his riches in glory by Christ Jesus.

Isaiah 28:13 But the word of the LORD was unto them precept upon precept, precept upon precept; line upon line, line upon line; here a little, [and] there a little; that they might go, and fall backward, and be broken, and snared, and taken.

2 Corinthians 3:18 But we all, with open face beholding as in a glass the glory of the Lord, are changed into the same image from glory to glory, [even] as by the Spirit of the Lord.

Romans 1:17 For therein is the righteousness of God revealed from faith to faith: as it is written, The just shall live by faith.

Hosea 4:6 My people are destroyed for lack of knowledge: because thou hast rejected knowledge, I will also reject thee, that thou shalt be no priest to me: seeing thou hast forgotten the law of thy God, I will also forget thy children.

Matthews 25:21 His lord said unto him, Well done, [thou] good and faithful servant: thou hast been faithful over a few things, I will make thee ruler over many things: enter thou into the joy of thy lord.

About the Author

James Freeman has a Master's Degree in Social Work from the University of Pittsburgh and a Bachelor's Degree from Washington and Jefferson in Psychology and Religion.

James has also earned a certificate in Child Welfare Studies from the School and Social Work and the MBA Essentials for Executive Leaders from the Katz Business School both at the University of Pittsburgh. He has been working with children and families, Para Professionally and professional for more than ten years. As a result of his desire to impact families in the urban community, James has sought work with faith based and community non-profit organizations.

He has advocated for families and children in several different arenas: James has worked as an in home service worker, foster care caseworker, trainer, mental health coordinator, social work administrator, and non profit senior executive. All these experiences have helped to provide a holistic view of how families operate and function under different circumstances.

James continues to work in the community. He is very active in his church activities at The Higher Call World Outreach Church. He serves as an Elder and works closely with the church leadership training and development team. His love of singing and worship to God keeps James close to the churches music ministry. James is over the praise and worship team and works with the church choir.

After serving as the Executive Vice President of the Nations leading kinship foster care agency, James has launched a faith based & human services consulting company. James is very concerned with the changing culture of child welfare services and the services provided to poor families and children. In addition, he is concerned with the child welfare workforce. His goal is to continue to provide resources and services that encourage, empower and engage commitment to quality clinical social work in the community.

James is a family man. He is married to Lachelle C. Freeman M.A., and the father of two children, Joshua and Madison Freeman.

For more information and booking, contact James Freeman at:

JTF95, Inc.
PO Box 17516
Penn Hills PA 15235
www.jtf95.com